*Jungian Reflections on
Literary and Film Classics:
opus 1*

AMERICAN
BEAUTY

*Jungian Reflections on
Literary and Film Classics:
opus 1*

AMERICAN
BEAUTY

by

Richard Chachere

CYPREMORT POINT PRESS
Lafayette, LA 70505

COPYRIGHT © 2003 BY RICHARD CHACHERE
ALL RIGHTS RESERVED

No part of this book may be used or reproduced in any manner whatsoever without written permission from the Publisher, except in the case of brief quotations embodied in critical articles and reviews.

Library of Congress Cataloguing-in-Publication data
Chachere, Richard
Jungian Reflections on Literary and Film Classics, Opus 1, *American Beauty*
p. cm.
ISBN 0-9740482-0-8

FIRST PRINTING

Jacket design by Mark R. Bacon and Gregory A. Melancon
Book design by Mark R. Bacon
Photographs by Richard Chachere
Author photo (back cover) and "Zorba" (page 26)
　　photographs by Terri Fensel
Printed in the United States of America on acid-free paper.

Published by Cypremort Point Press
P.O. Box 51705
Lafayette, Louisiana 70505

*Dedicated to my mother,
Helen Celia Beaullieu Chachere,
who taught me more about roses and what they mean about life,
than anyone could possibly imagine.*

*And to Jack Sanford,
whose brilliant interpretation of my archetypal rose dream
set me off on a great adventure.*

Table of Contents

1. Reflections on the Film — 1
2. The Dysfunction of American Relationships — 19
3. Paying Attention to Ourselves — 39
4. Defining the Heroic or Redemptive Personality — 55
5. Finding Our Way Through — 75
Glossary — 93
About the Author — 95
Bibliography — 96
Index — 98

Dreamworks Pictures presents
A Jinko/Cohen Company Production

AMERICAN BEAUTY

Theatrical Release in 1999

Screenplay by Alan Ball
Directed by Sam Mendes

Starring:

Kevin Spacey	Lester Burnham
Annette Bening	Carolyn Burnham
Thora Birch	Jane Burnham
Wes Bentley	Ricky Fitts
Mena Suvari	Angela Hayes
Peter Gallagher	Buddy Kane
Allison Janney	Barbara Fitts
Chris Cooper	Colonel Fitts

❧❧❧❧❧❧❧❧❧❧

Bruce Cohen	Producer
Dan Jinks	Producer
Alan Ball	Producer
Stan Wlodkowski	Producer
Debra Zane	Casting
Conrad Hall	Director of Photography
Thomas Newman	Soundtrack

Preface

Many thanks to the following members of my creative team: Rebecca Mills, first and foremost, my secretary and general "girl Friday," who tried to keep me on track. Lou Daleen, who transcribed my lectures and edited them, with a careful attention for Jungian concepts. Judy Beaullieu, my cousin/muse who first encouraged me (insistently) to see the movie.

To the one and only Geraldine Hubbell, multi-tasker and talent-pool extraordinaire, who insisted on publication, got all of these balls rolling and who introduced me to Mark Bacon, my art director, editor, general Godsend, and the bona fide professional of our group.

My dear sister, Celia Foard, who lent essential material support as well as "rose" back up.

My many clients whose stories have helped enrich this material. My dear *Acadiana Friends of Jung*, for whom the original lectures were formed and delivered, and whose reactions, comments and criticism helped give birth to these efforts. These friends have been the source of more than they could ever know.

Last, but not least, to Susan O'Neal, my life companion, whose support, encouragement, solid love and patience made these efforts possible.

Introduction

Dreams were very important to Carl Jung. They represent a very important aspect of every Jungian therapy and so are a constant emphasis of Jung. For an extraverted culture like the USA, nocturnal, imaginary dreams can be hard to come by. Pressured by work, ever increasing busyness, terrorist-driven economics and worship of technology and the internet, "night-time" is often found only in the *Phantom of the Opera*.

Every now and again, along comes a movie that seems to speak to the psyche of America. In 1999 the film, *American Beauty* seemed to do that. A dream about America and its family life. It is important to remember however, that dreams are symbolic, not literal, according to Jung.

This film is not about the disintegrations of the literal American family, but rather, about what can go wrong in the psyche of the participants and members of that family.

This book is the outgrowth of my lectures originally given to the *Acadiana Friends of Jung* in Lafayette, LA and elsewhere, exploring that dream film. Various groups have listened and responded and hopefully found the material lively enough to appear here.

I offer a couple of suggestions. Obviously, seeing the movie before reading this book would help. Actually, the lectures were given with the video clips of the movie illustrating each chapter. You might want to rent the video and read along with it.

Secondly, I use music a great deal in my lectures, to set a "tone," usually a "feeling" one to illustrate and accompany the material. For example, Giuseppe Verdi's great opera *Nabucco* is used throughout here. Strangely enough, even though far away culturally from the movie or *American Beauty*, in contrasting with it, affected a desired effect.

Playing music—and, in this case, the music of the chapters can be a way of meditatively preparing yourself for the material. Thus used, it can serve as your personal "retreat" or reflective seminar alongside and accompanying the vision this profound "American dream" constellates in you.

Happy dreaming,
Richard Chachere

Chapter 1

Reflections on the Film

JUNGIAN PSYCHOLOGY is called depth psychology, and it is called that because it is about the depths, about what is below the surface of things. The way one touches the depths is to go down, to go into the depths of one's self, and to go into the depths of life. That is an area where one doesn't exactly clamor to get to because it is scary. In fact, most of us have spent a lot of time pushing the depths away. So I would like to invite you to remember what we are about. It is about "going down" into the depths.

Our whole culture promotes "being up," "going up," and "staying up," so this going down means going against the grain. Even so—to risk it, to go against the grain—it is amazing to discover how just touching your own depths can make you feel better. You don't even necessarily have to do something. You don't have to heal yourself. You just have to go there. Just go there and you will find that our depths are so delighted to get a little attention that it is like a big Italian party. Verdi's music has that spirit. In Verdi's opera, *Nabucco*, do you remember the psalm the Jewish refugees prayed? "Out of the depths I cry unto you, O Lord." That is like the depths of ourselves clamoring for our attention. If we pay attention, we free them—and ourselves—from captivity.

In the movie, *American Beauty*, red roses are "the deal," the central image getting lots of attention. There is literally a rose named "American Beauty" around which a lot of things revolve in this fantasy. What became immediately clear from the strong reactions to this movie, is that this fantasy touches the shadow side of American family life.

There have been so many reactions to this movie, it has amazed me. Many people have sent me reviews and I have read different ones myself, but most of the reviews unfortunately only told you the obvious. That is not very deep and certainly not very new. Some deeper questions could have been asked: "Why does the movie grab people, and why does it have that energy? Why does it have such a 'POW!' effect and why did it win an award?"

I want to acknowledge that not everyone is wild about this film. In a way it is very dark and cynical. It devalues much that we hold dear as "American:" no virtues, no warm family life. It is not a "Loretta Young" or "Walt Disney" kind of fantasy, no "happily ever after" endings. In fact, it is "disaster ever after." The unfortunate thing is, it is true. It happens. It is a fact of modern life.

I think that the writer, Alan Ball, got it. According to the way he has described the experience of writing it and the making of the movie, I would say he got it almost straight from the unconscious. He has said in interviews: "The script wrote itself. It was as if the story had a life of its own and all I had to do was transcribe it." That description is always a sure clue that something else is involved, and if you are lucky, it is bigger than you. If you are "on," that is to say, on target and open and cooperating with it, it will be straight from the creative unconscious.

That is the constant task in creative work, to become an agent of something bigger than yourself. In fact, it's what this journey is all about. How do you do that? By tuning into yourself. By finding your center. You don't have to go to Hollywood. You don't have to imitate Alan Ball. You have to ape *yourself*. Everyone has creative work to do, a creative task. If you don't do it, your life is going to curl up on you—it is going to attack you—it is going to get sour. *You have to do your creative work—that makes all the difference.* I want to emphasize that. It is really important to "tune in" to your creative energy. Even if you just write in your journal fifteen minutes a day of what you see, it will make a difference. If you cut your pink roses in your garden, you will see what is important, because you are giving form to what only you see. It doesn't have to be filmed. It doesn't have to be seen by others at all—only by you and by God. It is also important to make a distinction, that by "creative," I don't mean "artistic"—that you have to become an artist all of a sudden. Creative means whatever in your realm gives you energy and where it is coming from.

Alan Ball experienced that in writing *American Beauty*. He also said that eventually the film began to acquire its own life, "just as the screenplay had when I was writing it. But then we changed things. Scenes were changed; some lost out and were scratched altogether. It was like the movie was letting us know what it wanted to be. He adds, "When the script was turned to film, it became a better film than the script I wrote." That is an extraordinary thing for a writer to say.

Ball continues, "What started out as a satire eventually revealed itself to be something entirely different and much more interesting, and I can't begin to claim credit for that. That is how you know when your story starts taking you—when your interest starts taking you somewhere." He contrasts this with our prevailing culture, packaging experience quickly so that it can be sold. In his screen notes and interviews, Ball has simply described for us the depth of his creative experience, and for which he won an award for Best Original Screenplay.

Do you remember the basic characters in the story? The Burnham family: Lester, Carolyn, and their daughter, Jane? They are in a deep state of alienation and not doing well, to put it mildly. Then there is the charming couple next door—the Colonel and his zoned-out wife, Barbara—and their son, Ricky. There is Angela, Jane's friend, whom Lester flips over, and Buddy Kane, the "real estate king," whom Carolyn flips over. So there is a lot of archetypal energy going on beneath the surface in these families.

The question arises, which of the characters is the most well-drawn in the film? During the lecture series, many voted for Lester. Remembering the story and the development of its main characters, I would have to say that Ricky is the most well-drawn in my opinion. Of all the characters in the film, he is the one who has a standpoint. As the film unfolds, he is the one with a point of view. He is the one who sees things and people very clearly. Furthermore, in my view, he was an absolute hero for handling his difficult father in such a creative way. Any person with a small ego living under that roof would have been run over. Just smashed. Not only did Ricky survive, he showed his father that he could make a thriving living. Even if it was on the shady (shadow) side, hidden, and someone like his father might call him "nothing but a drug pusher," Ricky made a living. Always taking the time to notice things, he said the line that is the title of the film: "Things are beautiful in life. When you see something like that, it is like God is looking right at you, just for a second. And if you are careful, you can look right back at Him."

That is pretty good for a "drugged-out hippie." You would think that he might see everything as flat, drugged out, zoned out—with his mother's eyes, Barbara's eyes. The Colonel comes in and beats him, bullies him. Yet he keeps on going, and he notices things, alert to what beauty there is in life.

That really stands out in one scene in the film. Ricky is talking to Jane as they are watching his video on the big screen in his room. He is describing the scene of a white plastic bag:

"We are in an empty parking lot on a cold, grey day. Something is floating across from us. It is an empty, wrinkled, white plastic bag. We follow it as the wind carries it in a circle around us. Sometimes whipping it about violently or, without warning, sending it soaring skyward, then letting it float gracefully down to the ground." "It was one of those days when it is a minute away from snowing. You can almost hear it, right? This bag was just dancing with me, like a little kid begging someone to come play with it for fifteen minutes. That's the day I realized there was this entire life behind things and this incredibly benevolent force that wanted me to know that there was no reason for me to be afraid, ever."

Not bad. In fact, Jung couldn't have put it better. In *Modern Man in Search of a Soul*, Jung said it this way:

"What I mean to convey is a human quality, a kind of deep respect for facts and events, a respect for the secret of human life. The truly religious person has this attitude. He knows that God has brought all sorts of strange and inconceivable things to pass and seeks in the most curious ways to enter a person's heart. He therefore senses in everything the unseen presence of the divine will." (p.234)

Ricky sees it. In everything. Not just the good stuff...not just the church stuff...not just the holy stuff, but also "almost hearing it" in a throwaway white plastic bag dancing in the wind. Ricky says, "That was the day I realized there was this entire life behind things." Talk about depth. "This incredibly benevolent force wanted me to know that there was no reason to be afraid, ever," Ricky said. Then humbly he adds, "Video is a poor excuse, you know, but it helps me to remember. I need to remember."

We all need to remember. We need to put it down, in writing, in video, on paper. We need to remember in those moments when everything is falling on our head or when Jupiter is shaking his finger at us when he is all riled up in the skies, when he is giving you "what for" about your life and how it has not measured up, etc. You need to be able to remember. You need to be able to go to your video, or your journal, or your poetry.

I saw a wonderful poem in the local paper. A little boy from Lafayette Middle School won the poetry award with his poem about going crabbing. The poem is so wonderful. You need to be able to remember moments like that. That is what the saints were for; that is what statues are for; what art is for. To be surrounded by something bigger, so that we can all remember. We are all shrunk down at times. We don't "have it."

But Ricky gets it. Ricky says the line that is the kicker: "Sometimes there is so much beauty in the world, I feel like I can't take it all in. Like I can't take it and my heart is going to cave in." Hearing that, Jane sees Ricky in a new way. She takes his hand. Up until that moment, Jane has bought the gossip line at school: "He's a weirdo." She is repelled. "Look at him. He's got this camera. He's looking at me." So she asks him, "Why are you doing that? Why are you looking at me?" Ricky replies, "Because I like you. Because you are interesting." Jane is only annoyed: "Well, stop doing it." Ricky simply responds, "O.K. I'll stop." (And he does). She didn't expect that. "But he looks weird and has that father."

So, my vote is for Ricky who gives us a viewpoint. He also gives us a special view of Lester and Carolyn, Jane's parents.

American Beauty is a very American film and it is very American about the disaster of married life. It is also the all-American Jungian mid-life crisis film. In the story, Lester is having his mid-life crisis, and sure enough, the *anima* comes and pops him on the head. He looks stupid. He especially looks stupid to his daughter, Jane: "I need a father who is a role model, not some horny geek boy who is going to spray his shorts whenever I bring a girlfriend home." What charming, good old American language. Indeed, the language in this film, as well as the language in America today, is rather coarse and harsh, symptomatic of when the center no longer holds, when there is so much disorientation. This always happens at these crisis times, life turns coarse and harsh. (cf: T. S. Eliot, *The Waste Land*; Edward Edinger, *Archetype of the Apocalypse*)

The story opens with Carolyn in the front yard gardening, with her American Beauty roses that are all snippety-snip-snip and in order and perfect. The *animus* couldn't raise roses any better. That is how they look. Sterile. All in a row. So perfect that you want to puke. And Lester does. He is married to this furious, irritating, raging woman. The result is that Lester and Carolyn give play to everything about the anima and animus duo in a terrible negative nutshell. She is everything a man doesn't need. Lester's view of her is captured in the perfect yet coarse comment he makes to Jane during one of their charming family meals:

> "…and your mother seems to prefer that I go through life like a fucking prisoner while she keeps my dick in a Mason jar under the sink."

Very well said. That is what happens and Lester has had it. He has been sleepwalking while Carolyn has been doing her jackhammer number on his head and other body parts, proving that he is totally dispensable. She goes so far in the rest of the movie to talk and act as if he weren't there.

In the realm of our human animal life and instinctuality, one thing the male needs is self-esteem and a feeling of confidence and support. This movie describes perfectly and archetypally what happens when a relationship goes down Bitter Street. The wife is stuffing her feelings and getting more resentful and bitter by the day, angry with him. He is being shut down more and more into this passive Mason jar container where nothing works.

Not surprisingly, something is going to have to explode. Sure enough, it happens when Lester and Carolyn attend a high school function for Jane—an event orchestrated, of course, by the wife, because Jane is "just dying" for them to be there. (Jane, of course, has been puking right and left on both of them, and couldn't care less if they would both disappear from the planet.) It is here that Lester sees Angela for the first time. Then we have roses that are a little more interesting than the ones in Carolyn's garden in the opening scene. We now have rose petals.

ಲ ಲ ಲ ಲ ಲ ಲ ಲ ಲ ಲ

The rose is the flower and symbol of Aphrodite (Venus)—the goddess of love and sexuality. Throughout the film, Angela is

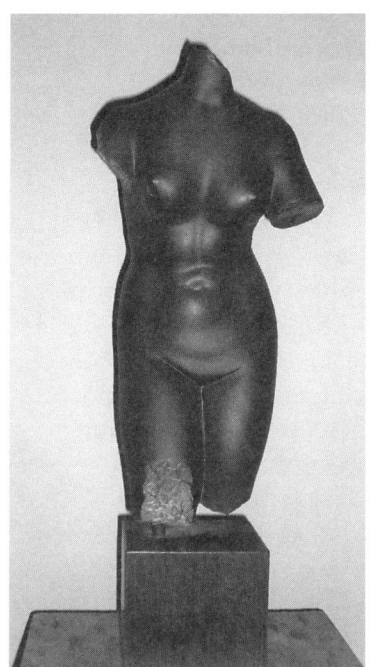

Statue of Aphrodite

imbued with these petals in Lester's fantasy life. While Angela is young and attractive, only someone like Lester—who has been so unconsciously grabbed by this projection—could see the divine in this young woman. This proves painfully clear in the their awkward love scene when finally, to our immense relief, the projection falls away. He is embarrassed. She suddenly feels stupid. That is what you get when a projection falls and crashes. All of a sudden you get this bitter taste of reality and often enough, it is not very pleasant.

There is a wonderful bumper sticker I saw recently: "Reality is for those who lack imagination." Unfortunately, it is one of those "either-or" statements. We need both. Hopefully all of us have imaginations and some of us have a little reality as well, because both are important. It is an awakening kick to see your own projection fall away, but that falling-away is very essential to both reality and imagination. It is really important when we are possessed by something.

In this case, Lester really *needed* the projection, because once he fell for Angela, he woke up. He says at one point in the film, "It is like I've been in a coma for twenty years and I am just now waking up." That is the one thing Angela does, or more precisely, it is the one thing the anima does—she wakes a man up. (Angela, the person, didn't do anything.) The anima may wake him up into looking very foolish to every hard nose around, but it is vital that he awaken.

Similarly, Buddy, the realtor, becomes important for Carolyn. There is an opposite flow of energy. The animus in Annette Bening's character, Carolyn, gets projected onto the realtor, and she tries to find some meaning in her existence.

However, I think the story of Lester is more well-drawn in the film, because it shows how the anima works for a man, even though it is often not appropriate, often not acceptable, and sometimes publicly embarrassing and disgusting. It works. You could say psychologically that it works for Lester because Angela is so young, and he needs to get kicked into gear. He needs to get his youthful energy back. These are the dynamics between Carolyn and Lester, and the unconscious animus and anima projections and conflicts they play out in the film.

✿✿✿✿✿✿✿✿✿

Then there is the Colonel. If you ever want to see Jung's theory of the shadow perfectly portrayed, it is the Colonel's role in the movie, and the evil that the shadow acts out in his character. We are introduced to him when the Colonel and his family move into the neighborhood, and are welcomed by their neighbors who happen to be two gay men. The Colonel comes to the door barely breathing, or breathing fire, and you have no idea what is going to happen, except there is an undercurrent of terror and rage underneath. He is seething.

The Colonel stares at the men suspiciously, believing them to be salesmen. He introduces himself: "Colonel Frank Fitts, U. S. Marine Corps," and shakes their hand only dutifully. Both men are named Jim, though one calls himself J.B. (for Jim Berkeley). Jim introduces himself, and J.B. as his partner, and both are trying to be cheerful and jovial, but the Colonel isn't responding:

> "Let's cut to the chase, O.K.? What are you guys selling?"
> "Nothing. We just wanted to say 'hi' to our new neighbors."
> "Yeah, yeah, but you said you are partners, so what is your business?"

The two Jims look at each other and then back at the Colonel: "Well, he's a tax attorney and I am an anesthesiologist."

The Colonel looks at them confused. The scene changes and the Colonel and Ricky are driving away. The Colonel says,

> "How come these faggots always have to rub it in your face? How can they be so shameless?"
> "That's the whole thing, Dad," Ricky replies, "They don't think they have anything to be ashamed of." (There's Ricky again, cutting right through it).
> The Colonel cuts a questioning look at Ricky, who quickly adds, "Yeah. You're right."

The Colonel's eyes flash angrily, "Don't placate me like I am your mother, boy."

"Forgive me, sir, for speaking so bluntly, but those fags make me want to puke my fucking guts out." (Ricky steps right in line and salutes the Colonel).

"Me too, son. Me too." Dad is placated. How thick can it get?

So what is the Colonel raging about? Homosexuality. It turns out at the end of the movie that he has been terrified all along of his own tenderness. And, of course, we don't know who pulls the trigger and shoots Lester, but the number one suspect is the Colonel, since he did have blood on his T-shirt at the end. That is what happens with the shadow. You hate what you get furious at and what you repress. You rage about what you don't deal with in your own life. The Colonel is the living, despicable carrier of that in the film. He beats his son. He forces him to give urine samples every six weeks. Meanwhile, the place of honor in his gun rack is given to a Swastika plate from the Third Reich. Merely touching the plate and showing it to Jane earns Ricky another beating.

Throughout the film, the Colonel's wife, Barbara, tragically looks like she has had a lobotomy. This is what happens in an atmosphere of that much repressed rage. It does not go away. The women become its victims. The toll is on Ricky's mother's face. It is the price the feminine and women wind up paying over and over.

The Colonel represents the repressed masculine hostility and rage that can't deal with its own tenderness and its own sexuality. Sexuality is right under the sheets all through this movie because it is about the shadow side of American family life. It is not very pretty.

☙☙☙☙☙☙☙☙☙

Today, my dog Gus and I were out in the yard checking the bees—the queen had been returned to the hive and we were out there to observe. Later, while I was at my desk writing some of these notes, I began to smell an unpleasant odor, as if Gus had left a calling card somewhere. I was totally immersed in my imagination, in writing this material, and yet I began smelling and smelling this odor. I went to look in the mirror to check my being, but I could not discover the source. Then as I came back to the desk, there it was, all over the floor, as I had stepped in it. I think it is a good metaphor for Lester in the film, because obviously there had been a big stink in his life for a long time and he didn't get it. All of a sudden he stepped in it. I think that is what happens when we go into a deep freeze about our emotions, about what we do not own in ourselves, do not see, and do not find.

Lester is a remarkable example of that in the film. The anima, played by Angela, is preposterously disconnected, which approximates the state of an American male's anima development. Lester is in his forties, Angela is sixteen. That is a huge gap. That is also what happens with fantasies. The imagination can do wonderful things, but unfortunately and sadly, it always needs a test of reality and appropriateness. It helps even more to get the level right. The anima is an inner reality. When she gets projected out, she causes great messes.

To his credit, Lester manages to have the fantasy—to not shut it off, nor judge it or kill it in himself. That is important because at that point in his life, he needed this fantasy to bring him to life. As he gets closer to Angela in the love-making scene toward the end of the movie, the obvious difference between his fantasy and her reality is enormous.

As it turns out, she has contributed to the gap between fantasy and reality. The difference between her fantasy and her reality is enormous because throughout the movie, she has been behaving like "Miss Sexpot", adopting an adolescent pose of worldliness. In reality, she is inexperienced, admitting to Lester—only at the crucial moment—that this is her "first time?'. The connection between them—where he has had this glorious fantasy life about "gorgeous Angela"—comes face to face with the reality of it all in one telling encounter.

In the Burnham house, Angela and Lester are together. She smiles. They stand in silence, the atmosphere charged.

"Jane and I had a fight," Angela tells Lester. "It was about you."

Angela is trying to be seductive, but she is pretty bad at it. That is when a man may begin to notice the difference between the anima and a real woman. You "hear" the difference. The anima is great at seduction, while an ordinary flesh and blood woman isn't, necessarily. You may remember this is Angela's great fear, as she told Jane and the crowd at the high school: "There is nothing worse in life than being ordinary!" She is quickly on a path to sail right out of that ordinary reality.

"Jane is mad at me because I said I think you are sexy."

Lester grins. "Do you want a sip?" offering her a beer. "So," he adds, "are you going to tell me?"

Now, there is the man's part of it. "Are you going to tell me?" He's there with a head loaded with fantasies. Right? And he asks, "Are you going to tell me what I want to hear? Are you going to tell me how you know exactly what I am thinking? Are you going to tell me how you are going to live out my fantasy? Do you get it?" This is Lester's first encounter with Angela and the first thing he says to her is: "So, are you going to tell me?" The reality is that she is sixteen. Of course she doesn't get it.

She asks, "What?"
Lester replies, "You don't know?"

Here is the other big giveaway about a man's psyche. He is sure that she knows and has been having those fantasies with him. But she doesn't have a clue.

This is really important for women to understand. Little girls are raised to believe "in sugar and spice and all that's nice." And many times, in this culture, women from childhood carry that belief unconsciously into their adult lives. They are taught to be that fantasy for men. However, there comes a time in a woman's life where she has to decide if she is going to spend the rest of her life being the "Snickers Girl" for men, or if she is going to carry herself. In other words, is she going to be the little carhop at the drive-in that is always running to bring the goodies for the guy, or is she going to be herself? This does not mean that she has to put him down or turn into a witch who uses coldness to turn the whole state of Louisiana into the North Pole. That's not it either. But when a man asks or says to her, "You don't know?" that is a giveaway that he is all into his fantasy stuff about her. That's just it. It is *about* her, it is *not* she. There is a vast difference. Do you see what I am saying?

"You don't know?" Lester says.

His face is very close. She is unnerved. This is happening too fast. This is a test of "little Miss Sexpot," and she starts crumbling. "Wait a minute…Oh, God, he took me seriously."

Well, what did you expect Angela, sweetie? That is when the women's awareness has to click in.

Angela asks, "What do you want?"

Lester answers, "Are you kidding? I want you. Don't you know you stupid little girl? I've wanted you since the first moment I saw you. You are the most beautiful thing I have ever seen."

"Can't you see my erection?" Lester might say. He is acting like a dog as it is!

❧❧❧❧❧❧❧❧❧

Michelangelo just took a dive (as did a few other classical artists of beauty) and Angela is the most beautiful thing on the planet for him in his "possessed" state. He wants to have sex with her. Period. This is a point in time when you know that we are dealing here, not with a human being, but with a goddess, according to Lester, who has made ordinary 16-year old Angela into a goddess. *When a man projects a goddess on a living woman, the woman is in trouble and the man is in even more trouble.* It just doesn't work. As Jack Sanford, the renowned Jungian analyst says so eloquently in *Invisible Partners*, love is a thing about two ordinary human beings and if gods and goddesses get mixed up in the equation, it falls to you-know-where (hell) and Lester continues on the downward slide to disaster: "You are the most beautiful thing I have ever seen and from the first moment I saw you, I wanted you."

At this point, Angela takes a deep breath and knows she is in way over her head. He kisses her cheek, her forehead, her eyelids and her neck.

"You don't think I'm ordinary?" she asks. That is where she hangs out. Sixteen. High school.

Lester answers with the classic male line: "You couldn't be ordinary if you tried."

One knows that when you get into this kind of dialogue, it is really embarrassing for everybody. "You couldn't be ordinary." Yes, she could. And just watch. She is going to promptly do just that. "Oh, thank you. I don't think there is anything worse than being ordinary." Lester kisses her. They are both into their romantic fantasies—he in his, she in hers, and Lester is going to be her "prince."

Meanwhile, Carolyn is driving her Mercedes. "I refuse to be a victim. I refuse to be a victim," she obsessively repeats to herself. She is into pop psychology and does not want to be done in. On she goes, pepping herself up ad nauseum. Of course that doesn't work, either.

Then we go back to Lester, who is unbuttoning Angela's blouse. The screen notes tell us that she "seems disconnected from what is happening." At that point, what else is a girl to do? Especially if she is not really there. She gets disconnected and splits off. Only then does she admit to Lester—

"I'm just sixteen and this is my first time."

Lester laughs (just like a man) and says "You're kidding?"

"No. I'm not kidding."

> He looks down at her, his grin fading, Angela lies beneath him, embarrassed and vulnerable. The screen notes from the film spell it out: "This is not the mythically carnal creature of Lester's fantasies. This is a nervous child." What a downer for Lester.
>
> Angela says, "I still want you. I just thought I should tell you, in case you wonder why I wasn't better."
>
> Lester's face falls. There is no way he is going to go through with this now, and Angela, carrying the projection, doesn't know what is happening again.
>
> "What's wrong?", she asks, "I thought you said I was beautiful. I thought you said I was the most beautiful thing in the world. Why is your face like that?"
>
> ("Oh, because I just got a taste of strong, cold reality, that's what he would say.") He grabs a blanket to cover her nakedness.
>
> He says to Angela, "You are so beautiful and I would be a very lucky man."
>
> He smiles and shakes his head, humiliated. Angela starts to cry.
>
> Lester says, "Don't." He hugs her, letting her put his head on her shoulder and stroking her hair and rocking her gently.
>
> "I'm sorry," she says.
>
> "You have nothing to be sorry about." But she keeps on crying.
>
> "It's. O.K.," he says. "Everything is O.K."

But not really. Everything is not OK. "Everything" has crashed. I think it is a wonderful scene because it certainly describes the difference, of coming to reality for a man, how his sexual fantasies get going and take him away from reality and how talking about it makes it, unfortunately, ordinary, which neither person wants in many cases. But it does make it ordinary. The Teenager's Nightmare.

This brings us to the whole uncomfortable area of sex. In Scott Turow's book, *Personal Injuries,* there is a wonderful scene with two most unlikely characters. I want to go over this scene with you to illustrate my point. The guy, Robbie, is a big-mouth shark character, a crook, "almost like" Italian Mafia, but basically a nice guy, despite his "job". Yvonne, an FBI woman jock, has been assigned to him, and she is tough as nails, tougher than he is, actually. It gets to be a question of what her sexuality is, really. He is trying to carry on with every woman he meets, and there is constant unpleasant friction between the two of them—she is mad at him most of the time, because she knows his motivation is strictly sexual.

In some kind of strange way , however, he gradually gets to be fairly decent with her. Meanwhile, he is trying "to set up" some crooked judges (who are doing fraudulent things) for the FBI, and Robbie is talking about Brendon, the big chief judge that they are after, who is really slick:

"You'd say he is charming, likable, poised, humorous, especially if you've got any power. Reporters, politicians, celebrities, anybody who can do him some good, he'll bark like a seal if he thought it would make you beholden. But when you get down through the layers, Brendon is an absolute asshole of a human being. Here, this will tell you something. I mentioned Costanza, Brendon's secretary, didn't I?" She remembered.

Robbie continues,
"To this day she is sitting right outside his office. She is a beautiful little lady, but listen how Brendon got his mitts on her. For twenty some years now, Costanza has been married. Costanza had better English than her husband, Miguel. She made it through secretarial school, but Miguel is a bus boy and after working around all the liquor he can steal, he is also a drunk. The world beats him, and he beats Costanza, and she is pouring out her woes to her boss, Judge Brendon. So, he is touching her bruises, and soon after, other parts. But Costanza is a Catholic girl of great virtue and Miguel is the hand of God that was dealt to her, so she cannot be bad with

Brendon and look her husband in the eye at night."
"So what does Judge Brendon do?" He acts very understanding, and of course, then the Department of Corrections offers Miguel a job down in Ridge Yard, about 300 miles away. He finds that his days off are on Monday and Thursday, and he can go home maybe once a month. Now Brendon has his way with Costanza, and never seems to notice (as Miguel does) that his side of the bed is still warm. And Brendon lets him notice. How can you not hate a guy like Brendon? Whenever Miguel comes by chambers to pick up Costanza, Brendon's number one thrill is to call her in for a little late dictation and get her to "honk his horn" while her hubby is on the other side of the wall, waiting. "Oh, Lord," Yvonne says. "Yeah," says Robbie, "and you think your sex life is strange?"

He was just talking now, but the remark hit her hard. She was afraid that he would put her down. "My sex life is not strange," she replied as she eyed him severely.

"Well, you're the only one on this *planet*. Sex is always strange, baby. Whether it is Brendon-strange, or me-strange, or you-strange—it is always strange."

She hadn't heard this theory yet.

"I mean this is the most private, the inner thing in life, isn't it?," he asked her. "It comes out just a little bit differently in each of us, like a fingerprint—who you do what with. And your fantasies (there's "the guy-thing" again) and what part you like best and what you are thinking about. It is unique. That is why it is intimate. That is why it can be like magic."

He took her silence to mean that she required convincing, so he kept on.

"Here is what I am saying. I picked up a woman one night that works in a clerk's office. Well, it was not really a pick-up. I have known her forever. She is a single gal—Joyce. Well, forget her name, but you know I like her. Anyway, we are both pretty toasted and we get to her place. She said, 'Sit down.' Then she takes out this photo album. She said she took all the pictures herself and they are all of her. She is doing a sort of strip tease for the camera, more like a tease, very explicit. I don't know if she sent this to the collected kinks of America or what. But she was ramping up to show it to somebody and it was I. You know, if I were a jerk, I would have laughed. But I was fascinated and very touched, also really turned on. And even though I wouldn't say she showed to advantage—she had pretty legs, but just about zip up top, and you know that camera can be pretty harsh. But she was sharing with me her strange little secret, which was cool."

He peeked her way to see how she had received this. "So," he concluded, "You might ease up on yourself. It is just strange where we all hang out!"

Not bad for ole Robbie. The point is, sexuality is a place where all of us do hang out, And it is a place where we often are not very comfortable and we aren't very free, especially if, we are like Costanza—good Catholic girls who have been trained in all that virtue and guilt. It is very hard to let all that rub off. It is even much harder if you are the Colonel, But the main point that I want to emphasize is that the fantasy part that accompanies it is very important, and we need to pay more attention to it. We need to be able to talk about it, because to talk about it brings it down to earth where it can be real or not, as Angela finds out and as Lester finds out. It is very important to deal with our fantasy life, to keep us from being up in the air and out there, and to bring it down to earth, or, for it to be perverted and make us feel perverted.

To move along then to the ending of the movie, I think Lester getting shot at the end was a cheap shot. It was "Hollywood," and I do not agree with it. I do not think that is the way he works it out. I think that if a person like Lester gets his act together, where he can retrieve his virility from under the sink, and back belonging to himself, and that if he can feel decent, about himself, stand up to Carolyn in whatever way even at a fast food drive-in, then it is really important. Life tends to honor that hard work in an individual. Jung would even call it consciousness. A man working out his masculinity. And redeeming it from passivity.

Jung says that when it comes to the animus in a woman, it always is going to test the nearest man—and the test is who's going to be the boss. Now, I want to make it clear that we are not talking about plantation days, and we are not talking about abuse or slavery. We are talking about who is going to be the man, and who is going to be the woman.

We are talking about who is going to be the leader and who is going to be not the follower, but the partner. If a man misses the charge, then it really goes sour. Obviously, Lester was too passive. He was asleep and Carolyn took over the show. It's not clear, despite her embarrassment and despite everything that happens to her, if it ever ends because "he" has her now. By that I mean the negative animus "has her"—the strong, pushy, go-get-em driving force that gets a woman and then doesn't let her stop once she psychologically identifies with "him"—meaning that inner inferior masculinity.

So it is Lester's sin that started it somewhere somehow. It is his penalty. It is his not measuring up to what she needed. Every woman knows deep down that she wants a man strong enough to stand up to her worst side. Not in brutality. Not in smart-assed-ness, not in sarcasm, but in honest, related strength that says you are not going to push me around like this because I have to have my honor. The tragedy of the film, in my opinion, is that it portrays a man totally without honor, at least at the beginning of the movie. Then, at the end of the movie, he finally gets his honor back, and they blow him away. I believe that is not the way it works. I think if you get your honor back, you don't die. You get to live. I think there are rules in the order of things and that it is to our wonderful advantage that Jung notated them for us moderns. These rules work in the natural order of life. One rule is, if you honor your soul, it honors you. It doesn't kill you off.

Those are my thoughts on this film. It is a film that perhaps may stimulate us into dealing with our own archetypes and relations, and to doing whatever it takes to work through them. It is to that task I now want to turn.

༺༻༺༻༺༻༺༻༺༻

Chapter 2

The Dysfunction of American Relationships

I SEE THE FILM, *American Beauty* as an American dream about the dysfunction of American relationships. It is symbolic of what goes on in relationships. Some of the topics I want to talk about in this context are:
- How to relate.
- How to see our fantasies about the relationship.
- How to gather our energies about our relationships, and how to keep the energy moving.
- How to be practical about our relationships between and among the sexes.
- How to recognize the two big archetypal figures, the negative anima and the negative animus, who get in the way and mess up relationships.

By now, you have been introduced to these last two, the negative anima and the negative animus, and how they played out in the characters of Lester and Carolyn in the film. Now I want to talk about how to recognize these two archetypes in real, every day, concrete life—how they sound in real, concrete conversation, and how they affect our relationships. There is so much to be gained if we get down to the nuts and bolts of this.

We need to learn to *listen* to our tone of voice. As we do so, we can make what is unconscious, conscious. We know how to spot the tone of a "bitchy woman" or a sarcastic, moody man, "when the boss is having a fit," or when the neighbor's wife is giving him hell. We need to hear how our tone of voice sounds when we speak. If you are a woman, you need to hear your tone of voice when you speak to a man, and if you are a man, you need to hear your tone of voice when you speak to a woman. It is also very important to hear how you speak to a person of the same sex. In fact, these questions are crucial in Jungian analysis. I think that, if done right, the majority of analytical work is pulling away the projections you have—particularly of the opposite sex—and seeing how all that works. In other words, you will spend hours and hours and dreams and dreams about Eros, about your relationships, and how you connect and how you disconnect. Dreams always bring up matters of relationships. In other words, you will become conscious of your relationships.

Appropriately, there were roses in our lecture room when this material was presented. These showed us an important point, that there is a *real* "American Beauty" rose. The whole problem about Carolyn in the movie was that her American Beauty roses were perfect. As we saw that night, most roses are not perfect. Some are fluffy, some are droopy. That is the difference between a projection and a reality. Real life is rarely perfect; usually it is ordinary. Projections tend to make loved persons perfect.

Now many of us crash in mid-life with a lot of projections of how it was *supposed* to be, how it was *supposed* to go. The fact is, by the time you reach mid-life you need to be past that, and if you aren't, something has happened. You have been on a space ship. You have been lying to yourself, or you have been making a career out of projections, which means—to be brutally honest about it—seeing everyone else's problems. Some of us are "career psychologists" like that. We are very good at analysing everybody else, but we couldn't see our own tics if we ran into them.

Well, life has a way of arranging that we will run into them- our own tics—eventually. The question is—and I assume that most of you are of good heart and good will—are we willing to look at ourselves? Are we ready and willing to look at our own relationships? Not comparing them to everyone else's, not blaming the other, but willing to hear and see ourselves? That is a real work of depth. I think that is where depth psychology has its greatest value.

Allow me to read some provocative quotes. The first one is from Jung:

"Besides the picture of the moon, I would like to place the spectacle of the starry heavens at night. For the only equivalent of the universe within is the universe without." *(Psychological Perspectives)*

Isn't that just like Jung, to turn it around on us? Just when everyone was ready for him to say that the only equivalent to the universe *out there*…but no, he says the only equivalent to the universe in here is that which you see out there. Just as I reach this world through the medium of the body, so I reach that world through the medium of the psyche. Jung says you reach this world by paying attention to the objective psyche.

Lester (played by Kevin Spacey) found out about that in *American Beauty*. He discovers the anima in living *American Beauty* color. Now the main thing that we need to know about the anima and the animus is that neither cooperates with human will power. That is why morality doesn't work very well when those two are involved. If you do not understand that point, then the film probably offended your sense of morality. That is why many people got mad at the movie, despised the movie, judged the movie, called it un-American or Communist-inspired (as Bill O'Reilly stated on Fox TV), or they walked out of the movie, snarling. Unfortunately, these people missed the point. The point was that these facts *happen*.

It does not matter whether it is pleasing, whether it is appropriate for an adult man to fall in love with a teenager, or whether it is appropriate or "just" for a guy who uses and sells drugs to escape from his "prison." It happens. Whether it is appropriate, whether it is moral, whether it is just, whether it is "American," it happens. Those are the psychic facts. The modern person will try to learn from the psyche. The modern person will not try to reverse that, to make the psyche learn from America, or learn from the church, because the psyche is the main teacher, and two very important teachers in the psyche are the *anima* and the *animus*. If a man doesn't get it, as Lester wasn't getting it, then the anima will move into high gear to wake him up. Then he has to do something or look like an ass—and probably he will look like an ass anyway, so he might as well do something about it. If you are a woman, the animus will do likewise. Van Franz, *The Golden Ass*, when she describes at length, the assedness of men and sex.

Here is a quote from Erich Neumann, in his book, *The Great Mother*:

"The anima is the mover, the instigator of change whose fascination drives, lures, and encourages the male to all the adventures of the soul and spirit of action and creation in the inner and outer world."

That is a big mouthful. Think about that. And, the animus does the same thing for a woman—the instigator of change, the fascination. It is no accident that both of these words—and their meaning—come from the Latin word that means "soul." So, this means that the anima and the animus are determined that you are going to have a soul. If you are all bland and blah, and a passive loser like Lester, then one day, the anima hits you and Bingo! You are smitten. Irrationally, stupidly. By a high school cheerleader, no less, and your daughter is puking and it is the last straw for your wife. Hello! A major wake-up call.

What we need to see is how your anima, if you are a man—or animus, if you are a woman—wants to get you into life. They want you to have a life. If you are not having one, they will do bizarre things to you. It depends on how bizarre your need is, but they are relentless in their determination that you get a life. The more you suppress that—the more you deny it, reject it, or don't have time for it—the more negative it gets, but it doesn't stop. Then you have someone like Lester, who "wakes up" at age forty, and this whole affair is entirely inappropriate. He is forty, and the girl is about sixteen, which tells us that is about the stage of development of his feminine side. It has been stuck there, not going anywhere, so he has some fast catching up to do, so to speak.

He has got to grow up on his feminine side. What does that mean? I think it means, in this case, that when Lester's anima is carried by Angela, a little sexpot teenager that is his feeling for his life. He begins to ask those questions, "What am I doing?" "What about my job?" "What about Jane?" "What about Carolyn?" "Where did this go wrong?" "Where did I go wrong?" At first, the answers he comes up with are appropriate for a teenager—all that youthful energy he needs. As the movie concludes, he has begun to grow up, to be related, but very painfully.

༺ ༺ ༺ ༺ ༺ ༺ ༺ ༺ ༺ ༺

Roses are very important in mythology and in the archetypes, and they just happen to be the mythological flower of Venus or Aphrodite, the goddess of relationships. Now roses are noted for having thorns as well as for having lovely colors and aromas, reminding us of the ancient saying "Where there is honey, there is also the sting." Where there is life, there are thorns. Where there is reality, there are thorns. Even perfect rose beds, perfect roses, and perfect stems do not get rid of the thorns. A lot of relationship issues are really about how real we want to be, and how our romantic illusions and projections carry us so far

Old fashioned "English" Roses

away that we can't stand to let go of them. It is interesting, that in developing hybrid tea roses—a type of rose" rose growers tried to develop the "perfect rose." But what they got instead, was a "hybrid,"—a man-made creature that is an ugly bush on a "flowering machine" which is very often disease and insect-prone.

The Rose is such a rich symbol—it literally has a "thousand faces." It is rich in its varied meanings and nuances, describing at once and yet again, the never-ending paradoxes of love. It is beautiful. It has thorns. We "love" it. "We can't live without it," and yet often, find it hard to live with it. Commitment, especially today, seems terribly "thorny" yet marriage has not gone out of style. Younger people seem "to live together" outside of marriage, all the while they seem to want marriage eventually. (cf: *"Why There are no Good Men Left–The Romantic Plight of the New Single Woman"* by Barbara Whitehead; 2003)

Roses come in all sizes and shapes. Some like "American Beauty" have this appeal. "Old fashioned" roses are gaining in popularity today. Does this signal that old fashioned love values are more esteemed today? There are some who would say so.

Roses carry the meaning of Eros, relationship. To learn to relate, to discover the many levels of relationships, is important. There are several levels to life, Jung brilliantly told us. First, the surface level—the most obvious—the literal level. Love as caring, for example, would be the obvious level.

Then there is the deeper level: "what is the meaning of such and such?" What does it mean, "to care for someone?" Then you get into deep water. Some people seem to have an aversion to deep water. They live on the surface of life, with all of the shallowness that implies. I once heard the ultimate disparaging remark about someone: "He (so and so) has all of the depth of a floating leaf." To my mind, the speaker could not have "put down" that person any lower than she did. She did not hold that person in "high" regard. Do you notice the play of "high" and "low" references?

Finally, there is the unconscious level—the symbolic one—what we could call the deepest level. It is that because it can open out to all sorts of meanings. What does it mean that the Rose is Aphrodite's symbol, her flower? It means basically, that love/lust is connected with the energy of Aphrodite. What does that mean? It means that energy and sexuality is often connected with connections! Jung once put it more eloquently: "We yearn for what we lack." By that he meant, our sexual attractions, our sexual fascinations can reveal to what we need for our further development. But because it has to do with the psyche, it has to be understood on the *right level.*

For example, if I'm married and I "fall in love" with another woman, it doesn't mean I must have an affair with her (although most people do. While our churches condemn it, meaning try to repress it). What it does mean however, is life is trying to force you to pay attention to something you *do not have* which *may be vital to your life?* You need the *quality* that that person *carries for you.* What is very difficult to understand, to experience, to grasp is that you do not necessarily need that person. You need the quality, the character, and the personal trait that person carries for you. And usually, upon closer examination, you will discover not only do you lack that quality, but also even more so, it is precisely that quality you need.

Let us say, "Elizabeth" is going through a bad time. She dreams (she is single in real life) that me meets a great guy "very cute" and they are having wonderful sex. Now it turns out "our dream lover" is "strong" and "clearheaded" and "stable"—precisely the qualities Elizabeth needs in her life right now. And the dream says, "those qualities" in the person of "Brad" are leading her into precisely what she needs. Isn't that wonderful? Dreams are like that. Attractions are like that. Fascinations are like that. Trying to tell us what we need to be bigger, to be healthier, more loving. Like Roses.

Aphrodite (feminists, take note) was not known for her "smarts." She was known for her seductive powers: that is what Aphrodite loves to "stir up." She was kicked out when Christianity came along and replaced Greek mythology, but she is taking her ferocious revenge in our time. (Just ask the Roman Catholic Church.) And I happen to think the film, American Beauty portrays some of that. Unfortunately, all of life has two sides, and so does Aphrodite. In her myth story, she has an affair with Ares, God of War (what does that mean about affairs?) and then leaves him when her angry husband Hephaestus catches poor helpless Ares. Sound familiar? What does this mean? At the very least, it means Aphrodite's been stirring around, that she loves to stir things up, but she leaves a lot of suffering in her wake. That is why there are so many timid souls who are terrified of love and its risks.

But as an antidote to that, listen to Edith Hamilton's quote about Aphrodite. The Romans had this to say of Aphrodite (*Mythology*, Page 33, par. 1)

> "With her, beauty comes. The winds flee before her and the storm clouds; sweet flowers embroider the earth; the waves of the sea laugh; she moves in radiant light. Without her there is no joy nor

loveliness anywhere."

She makes life lovely. She brings beauty to life. She brings color to life.

You see, the timid ones turn "grey." Isn't that an awful fate? So, if your life has been "grey"—meaning, depressed, without purpose, having a "what's the use" feeling, there is a good chance you have kicked Aphrodite out of your life.

A shining example comes to mind. When I had just begun practicing as a therapist, we had a noted Jungian analyst Gilda Franz from Los Angeles speaking here. After dinner, I took her for a walk to show her my newly planted "English rose" garden. Without missing a beat, Gilda turned to me and said "Richard, you have so much passion! How could you have ever been a Roman Catholic priest?" I was dumbstruck by the lightning bolt of her words. Thank goodness that now seems like "another lifetime" and "another life" ago.

In his *Dream Seminar*, Jung tells the wonderful Jewish legend of the *Evil Spirit of Passion*.

A very pious and wise old man, whom God loved because he was so good, and who had meditated much about life, understood that all the evils of mankind come from the demon of passion. So he prostrated himself before the Lord and begged him to remove the evil spirit of passion from the world, and since he was such a very pious old man, the Lord complied. And as always when he had accomplished some great deed, the pious man was very happy and that evening as usual he went into his beautiful rose garden to enjoy the smell of the roses. The garden looked as it always had, but something was wrong, the perfume was not quite the same, something was missing, some substance was lacking, like bread with no salt. He thought he might be tired, so he took his golden cup and filled with some wonderful old wine which he had in his cellar and which had never failed before. But this time the taste was flat. Then this wise man had in his harem a very beautiful young wife, and his last test was that when he kissed her she was like the wine and the perfume, flat! So up the roof he went again and told the Lord how sad he was, and that he was afraid he had made a mistake in asking to have the spirit of passion taken away, and he begged him: "Couldn't you send back the Evil Spirit of Passion?" And as he was a very pious man, God did what he asked. Then he tested it all again, and marvellously enough, it was not flat at all—the roses had a wonderful perfume, the wine was delicious and his wife's kiss was sweeter than it had ever been.

Early in this work, *Zorba* fascinated me in the sense that we talked about. For those of you unfamiliar with the story, it is Nikos Kazankakis' masterpiece about an uptight young man who needs "to learn to dance" in the words of Zorba. I saw the play (three times), read the book and bought paintings by Anthony Quinn. Several years later, a new client, a young lawyer much like the one in the book, came up the stairs to my office and saw the Anthony Quinn self-portrait as Zorba. He asked me, "Richard, could this be your portrait?"

"No," I burst out gleefully, and told him who it was. "But," I added, "You have made my life!" So I know this material works.

Zorba (and Anthony Quinn, who lived the role, often literally and disastrously) was an Aphrodite-filled man. Kazankakis showed us the power of passion in the young uptight lawyer's transformation at the hands of Zorba.

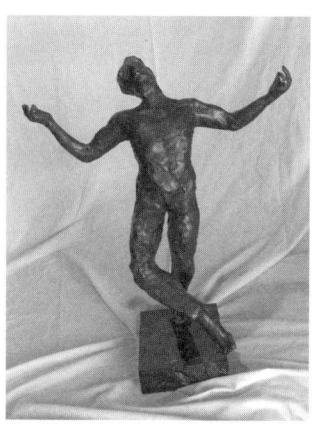
"Zorba's Dance" sculpture by Anthony Quinn (1983)

A final word about roses. They are "heavy feeders". In garden-talk, that means they need lots of fertilizer. Jung and von Franz, talk often and repeatedly about the symbolic meaning of "manure"—the rich fertilizing quality of our chthonic selves, meaning our earthy, instinctual side that is very akin to barnyard animals. It is the opposite of "the head"—of "thinking"—of being intellectual or rational. It has to do with our "lower down" instincts, like the gut, or spontaneous emotionality, or passion.

Those are the qualities that feed your psychic roses—which will indeed make your garden grow. Your life will be enlivened and beautiful rich colors (emotions) will fill your days.

> Life will be an adventure; It will not be grey or boring
> So tighten your seat belt!

But it is not cheap and it is certainly not free. You have to earn it the

The Hybrid Tea Rose, "American Beauty"

old fashioned way—through hard work.

I have a male client, a lawyer, who loves to talk about his white picket fence romanticism. Now when one thinks of a white picket fence, one sees a nice family, right? But the reality is that this man's life is all blown apart. Yet to this moment he has not let this illusion go, even at age 50. He is still clinging to the white picket fence, even though he is divorced and all kind of awful things have happened in his relationships with women. I told him, "It's not there. You can't have it. You can't have it anymore." Yet he argues, and gets sentimental, and asks, "Why not?" He argues "it is OK if it doesn't hurt anybody," and I reply, "What about you? It's hurting you."

This work of art almost could be a visual mantra for *American Beauty* and for us. It is a sculpture from London by Laurens van der Post's friend, Frances Baruch. It is called *Lazarus*...being raised from the dead. When I saw it, it really hit me. It is an image of the psychological work we do—that of getting the bonds off, and the necessity of breaking our projections. I see all of this bondage as

Lazarus, sculpture by Frances Baruch (1991)

projection, the stuff that holds us to death. It is the mother complex at its worst. It holds us back from having a life, from living, from facing the reality of what we have been given. It is so very powerful, I think. It certainly was for me, anyway. The soul lives through images. The soul makes images and resonates from images, and we need images to see. That is why movies like *American Beauty* can be helpful and stimulating for a lot of people. Marie-Louise von Franz once said that movies are like dreams for modern people. The movie captures the psyche at a certain moment if the audience is open to it. Done in that way, a movie can illuminate the moment.

As we "walk around" in this work about our relationships, I want to spur you on to get into your inner life, to listen to your inner dialogue, as well as to listen to your tone of voice when you are in conversation. *I want you to notice what happens in your conversations, to see the other person's face, to notice if they look like they have been hit.* Even if you didn't mean to hit them. Even though you meant well. Even if they are neurotic as hell and they should not be looking like they have been hit. The fact is, they have been hit. The facts. Stick to only that. Just look at the facts. Not to judge them, but to gather your information so that you can see this and can understand how it happens, how it operates in your own relationships.

Here is a great dream that Marie-Louise von Franz recorded in her series, *The Way of the Dream*. It touches on all of this and ties it together very well. It touches some of those deep places. This is a woman's dream. It is not a dream that Lester would have, though it could have been a dream that Carolyn might have had:

> "I dreamt that a woman was trying to see herself in a mirror. My husband has taken it away, so that he doesn't have to look at me. Her friend, who was a woman, said: 'My husband has done the same thing to me, and I could kill him.' Then there was the figure of a woman floundering in the sea, and a male voice said: 'She always used to swim naked like this early in her career.' It was Marilyn Monroe, luminous in white with her yellow hair spread out on the wave much like the calendar shot where her yellow hair is spread out on red velvet. The only problem was she didn't have any legs or arms, just her trunk. She seemed to notice that I was watching, and turned her whole torso toward me. It was just the trunk, sad looking, floundering in the water. I caught the expression of her mouth, which was painted in red but so sad, and I said, "She always turns when she knows that she is being watched,

hoping to catch desire in the eyes of sailors."

Well, what could you say about a woman who might have such a dream?

At the beginning of the dream is the strange disappearance of a mirror. A mirror is something in which we reflect. The mirror reflects our image. The word "reflect" has a double meaning—it means also to reflect upon oneself. To reflect means to think, to bend back upon oneself, to find one's own identity. And the mirror shows one's true face, objectively. Therefore, it is very often a shock to look at one's self in the mirror. If you think of the mirror in the fairy tale, *Snow White*, it tells the truth to the witch Queen. It tells the witch that Snow White is more beautiful than she, and the witch Queen gets furious. So the mirror is what shows the true reflection of ourselves.

Now in the dream, both of these women accuse their husbands of having taken away the possibility of seeing their own identity. Whenever we get into a relationship, that is always the first shot. It is *he (or she)* that did it. In our culture, this is what some members of the women's liberation movement say—that it is the men (or the patriarchy) who steal their identity. Unfortunately, for some women, the real problem is that they don't have their own identity. They feel raped or they feel that their own feminine identity has been stolen from them. That is a real feeling. The cheapest response though is to accuse the man (or men, or the patriarchy) because *that* takes the heat off the woman. However, the dream says the problem is this reflection in the mirror. Now, the husband may have contributed to this response because men naturally carry in themselves all sorts of romantic notions about the ideal woman. Those ideas generally come from "mother." If men love their mothers, then their women should be as much like their mothers as possible. If they hated their mothers, then their women should be as different from mother as possible. Women have a natural tendency to comply with the wishes of their surroundings and to relate personally to their surroundings—that is a feminine instinct. Therefore they often feel forced to play a role toward their husband or their man, to fulfil his expectations instead of being themselves. Naturally then, the women feel bitter, as though their husbands stole from them all possibility of being themselves. That is where the film, *American Beauty* opens, where Carolyn (played by Annette Bening) is full of resentment toward Lester.

Generally speaking, we can say that this resentment is usually a projection. It is a woman's own "inner" or unconscious masculine that has stolen her identity and it is her task to get it back—to get it back on her own and without blaming men. The loss of the mirror is actually the result of social life in general, and the plain result in the dream is a feeling of despair, of having lost the mirror, and with it, the ability to see oneself as one really is. Here then is this pathetic creature, Marilyn Monroe, still turning to catch the desire of men.

That is how women become their own worst enemies. They have been taught and trained from a very early age: "That is how you catch men, that is how you get a husband, that is how you get somewhere." There is unconscious role-playing that goes on all the time, just like in the dream, "turning to catch desire." Marilyn Monroe is a very ambiguous figure, because to millions of men, she played the ideal feminine image, yet she had trouble knowing who she was herself. She finally couldn't take it anymore; the clash was just too much. She lost the feeling of who she was in her private life.

It doesn't matter if you are a star, if you don't have a private life. It doesn't matter if you have a great job, if you don't have your own life. It doesn't matter if you have a lot of money, if you don't have your own life. It doesn't matter, doesn't matter, doesn't matter. You have to have your *own personal life*. Your children, your family, your status, your job, your career—none of these bring fulfilment within. Lester and Carolyn show us that in living color.

Marilyn Monroe had an obsessive fantasy, as von Franz points out in her analytical discussion of the dream. In her youth, Marilyn would fantasize that she was entering a cathedral and the whole congregation, which had been looking toward the altar, turned around and stared at her. Nobody looked at the altar; they just looked at Monroe. She was the goddess. Now, that means real trouble when you take the place of God. It brings real trouble when you identify with a role. It became real trouble for Marilyn Monroe and her identification with the goddess proved her undoing.

Learning to play the anima is begun very early in a woman. And learning to look for the anima begins very early for a man. These are the two great recipes for collision in mid-life when everything goes thud. You may wake up and say "Aha," or you may go through the motions like Lester, and one day say, "I have lost something, but I don't know what it is." What he lost was his real life. He sets out to try to find it and by the end of the movie, he is well on his way—that is, until Hollywood intervenes with its sorry ending.

The plan—the way through this—is to talk about these things, to go into more depth, and to try to get practical by asking these questions of yourself. If you are a man, "How do you start hearing your anima? How does she act? Is she in any way like Marilyn?" If you are a woman, "How do you start hearing your animus?" We are great about hearing it in others, but how does he sound in *your* conversations? "Do you ever hear it?" "Have you ever heard him?" And if you haven't, "How do you start to do that?"

The animus loves "should" and "pressure." You could say that the pressure voice *inside* a woman, the inner voice which is always after her (and others) to perform, to be a certain way, and to "should, should, should" is a great way to identify the negative animus. What about the anima? How does the negative anima sound? Many times, the anima in a man is sarcastic. What would be the comparable voice in the anima to the "should" and "pressure" from the animus? The anima is the "seductive" voice in a man, certainly, but it is also the "putting down" voice in a man. Its message is: "you are never going to get there," "you are not good enough," etc. It loves words like "never" and "nothing," reducing everything to zero. It is a discouraging, disheartening voice compared to the critical taskmaster animus voice in a woman.

To put it concretely, imagine the worst scene you can of a mother "jumping on" her son when he has screwed up terribly, and she is lambasting him. She then becomes identified with that animus critic and taskmaster, and her son interjects that voice and has it for the rest of his life. It is an inner voice calling him to task, undermining his self-confidence, and unless he has lots of *oomph* and can work past this in himself, he gets stuck right there and psychologically becomes a mother's son.

We need to reflect, to think about how the negative animus or the negative anima sounds in our own inner life. How does "he" sound? How does "she" sound? Chances are, we can find out how those sound by noticing our conversations and by watching the other person and his reactions. Even better, and more courageously, ask the other.

∽∽∽∽∽∽∽∽∽∽

I want to now talk about communication, and introduce a really helpful image for that communication as being a game of pitch and catch, where the idea is to keep the ball in play. The ball, because it is round can be a symbol of the Self. Therefore, when it is in play, it gives energy. Balls often appear in dreams. Therefore, when the Self is in play, the Self gives energy.

As in the game of tennis, the object is to keep it in play-to hit the ball back, and to respond to where and how the ball is hit to us, so that we can return it. However, unlike in a tennis match, the object is not to "win the game" with an un-returnable ace or an overhead smash. The object in communication is not to throw the ball at the person. Nor is it to drop the ball, nor to throw it away, nor to say, "I am not playing anymore"—which is what many of us do. To catch and respond means to keep the interaction of the twosome going. Communication is like that: it keeps the ball in play, but the focus is not on winning.

Jack Sanford has written a book called *Between People*, which offers very simple, basic and practical advice about this technique. It makes a huge difference if you remember this basic idea—to keep the ball in play and to do whatever it takes to do that. You may have to go "fetch" a lot. The other person may have thrown the ball out of bounds—way over there—or way over your head, and at this point, it depends on how related you are. Obviously, it also depends on how much the game of life means to you. That is very crucial because we all have little systems where we defend ourselves and rationalize. That stops the ball. That breaks the game. The task is to keep the energy flowing and the way to do that in a relationship is to keep the ball in play. Even if you have to eat a lot of crow, which most of the time involves the ability to apologize. You will need to learn to recognize when "that wasn't a very good throw," "that wasn't very catch-able," or when "that wasn't very nice," admit it and own up to it, so that the game can resume.

Someone from the audience has just volunteered a "foul ball"…"*the silent treatment.*" You hit the jackpot. That means dropping the ball, not keeping the ball in play. It takes many forms. Leaving the room. Sleeping somewhere else. A feeble excuse is given: "Time out." Giving the ball a rest? No, the Self does not need a rest. The relationship may need space, but the ball, the Self, doesn't. The Self wants to keep the energy of life flowing at all costs, *all of the time.* That is almost a given.

What is a common way of *not* handling the ball? Someone has suggested "arguing?" No. That is a way of keeping the ball in play, if it is a related argument between the two. Arguing is important. Conflict—learning how to have conflict and get to the other side of it is extremely important in relationship. In fact, there is no such thing as a relationship without conflict. If there is, something is really dead.

What are ways to *drop* the ball? One has been mentioned—the silent treatment. What about collusion or non-interest—not doing what it takes to keep things going? I think that one of the biggest ways to drop the ball is to say "*I don't know.*" There are any number of variations on the theme. "I don't know what I am doing." "I don't know what I mean." "I don't know what I am saying." "I don't know why I did that." What is really being said is, *"I don't want to be conscious about this."* And where does that leave the other person? Well, he cannot hit the ball back. The game just stops dead. If you think about relationships as keeping the ball in play, that motion can make a big difference because the energy continues to move.

It is very clear from the beginning of *American Beauty*, that there is no game at all between Colonel Fitts and his wife, Barbara. The game has long been over—she is dead. There is no game between Carolyn and Lester anymore, either. The only one who still has the ball in play is Jane, the daughter, and she wants to throw it at both of them. However, the game is over for the parents in both families and that is when things start deteriorating rapidly. The energy of the Self has to go somewhere. If it doesn't go into the game of life, and in the communication between them, it will go against them. That is an important concept to understand.

One of the big cop-outs is "That's not my problem." Or, "I don't want to go there;" "It's not going to go anywhere," "I don't want to talk about it," or "I don't like this conversation?" These are all good male cop-outs. "Why bother? This is too much trouble." That is saying "It is not worth it." *Wow*. Do you hear how lethal that is? If it is not worth it, then let's go home. Oh, we are home. Then you go, and I will stay.

You have to make it worth it. Unless, of course, you get a revelation like Lester did—"Hey, it is dead, it is in the coffin and it needs to be buried." Many people cannot bring themselves to go there, but the fact is, you need to be able to call a corpse a corpse. Otherwise you stay in the land of the dead and the land of the cop-out. "I don't want to talk about it." "You are too difficult". "This is all too much for me". Using these copouts is retreating from life—not playing the game. If you have someone in your life who retreats like that, what do you do?

When a relationship goes on like that for a long time, obviously the relationship becomes very difficult, often too difficult. The players lose interest in the game. The players may just give up, and quit playing. This is the sorry state *American Beauty* is lighting up for us, up close and personal. Lester is about to have a big anima affair, and Carolyn is preening to become the great Realtor of Suburbia. In the process she just happens to run into Mr. Real Estate himself. So both Lester and Carolyn are headed for Affairsville, with their anima and animus projections landing them in the soup. Neither of them knows where the ball is or how any of this will help the ball game. If you think of communication in that way (as carrying the ball) you will begin to hear those two characters—the negative anima and negative animus— a lot more.

Another very important image around this whole topic of relationship is an image used by Jung a great deal, called *participation mystique* which describes being *enmeshed* with one another, like a man and his dog in the dark. This is Jung's comment from his *Dream Analysis Seminars* in December of 1928 (p.63).

> "We have a great problem today because that collective, marital relationship is not what people expect of it—an individual relationship. And furthermore, it is exceedingly difficult to create one in marriage. Marriage in itself constitutes a resistance. This is simply a truth. For the strongest thing in man is participation mystique; just you and your dog in the dark; that is stronger than the need for individuality...."

For all of you optimists out there, this is not good news about creating individual relationship in marriage. He describes it as "just you and your dog in the dark," meaning, "I don't see anything. I just want to keep walking. We're having such a nice time, having a good walk. Don't make me think. Don't make me see anything." That's *participation mystique*. That is stronger than individuality. To want to become conscious, to become an individual, will be going—big time—against nature and against the grain. You are going to feel like you and your dog in the dark.

Jung continues:

> "You live with an object and after a while you assimilate each other and grow alike. Everything that lives together is influenced, one by the other. That is participation mystique."

I saw a good example of this with my dog Gus, an 80 pound, alpha male, golden retriever—a huge dog. Gus is dead now, but I told his breeder recently, "When I first got Gus as a puppy, I had a Boston terrier, Canille, and the terrier was the older, more dominant one. Huge Gus had to be submissive to the diminutive Boston terrier and he learned all of the Boston terrier's bad habits. Gus became an aggravating Boston terrier!" The breeder did not bat an eye. She replied, "Well, Gus took on the personality of the Boston terrier." I said, "Damn. You're right!" That's participation mystique—Gus and the Boston terrier.

If you are around somebody long enough, you become like him or her, whether you like him or her or not. Whether they are likable or not, you pick up their "stuff." This identity, Jung says, results when the "mana of one assimilates the mana of the other." ("Mana" is the power of what the other carries, the power of the personality.) "This identity" Jung says, "this clinging together, is a great hindrance to individual relationship." Gus couldn't be Gus as long as the Boston terrier, Canille, was there. He just couldn't.

Jung continues:

> "If identical in this way, then no relationship is possible. (Relationship is only possible when there is separateness.")

Separateness cannot exist unless you have two separate individuals. If they are both trying to become one, then they become enmeshed. And of course, that is what we are taught that marriage is supposed to be!

> "Since participation mystique is the usual condition in marriage, especially when people marry at a young age, an individual relationship is impossible."

That is a shocking and startling statement. That is why very often life comes along to break up that enmeshment. Unfortunately, when people do not understand what is going on, they bail out. They get divorced or they hate each other. Or they do as Lester, who runs off after the cheerleader, with no comprehension whatever as to what is going on, and with no comprehension of the deeper meaning of things. And sometimes, even though one does know the deeper meaning, one still does it. One has to do it. One has to live it out and learn it the hard way. Perhaps many of us have several doctoral degrees in that department- in living life the hard way. You know, "the hell with the books, the hell with the theories, full speed ahead." I am going to live my life then when you look back, what a cruise you have had.

Jung continues:

> "Perhaps the two hide their secrets from each other. If they admitted them, perhaps they could have established a relationship...."

That is very important. Secrets build barriers. Secrets destroy connections. That does not mean that a couple should have "true confessions" overnight but it *does* mean that trust is important. Playing games behind another's back is not going to establish a relationship. Jung then says:

> "Perhaps they have no secrets to share; then there is nothing to protect them from participation mystique. One sinks into that bottomless pit of identity and after a while discovers that nothing happens at all any longer."

On the other hand, having no secrets is no solution, either. One has to have life, otherwise what Jung says is fairly obvious—the bottomless pit of identity is not the ideal as we are taught to think. I know of one family where "togetherness" was the family theme song. Not surprisingly, that family eventually and violently blew apart.

This is quite a mouthful. The strong need for individuality is not as strong as the need for belonging and being connected. The individual relationship does not usually happen when you are young. I call it the second marriage syndrome. People get married young to propagate the species and then they get married again later on when they are half way, or at least pseudo-composed, half-cooked so to speak. Then they have a chance.

Participation mystique or clinging together is not conducive to separation. Being a separate entity or individual is a requirement to have a real relationship. Surprisingly, you can't do that if you are all enmeshed with somebody else. That is why typically in mid-life relationships, he has his life and she has her life, and they connect in the middle to share and enjoy it, but they do not duplicate each other. The two are beginning to have their own identities.

It is a truism that opposites attract, and if you really look at it, it is the conflict in a relationship that really keeps it alive. When you try to smooth all of that over, and make it peaceful, then you are either sleeping on a land mine, or you are killing all of the uniqueness. In *American Beauty*, when Lester wakes up, he discovers this terrible grey depression all around because life has been snuffed out. Individuality and uniqueness means that you are different. That seems too obvious, and I struggle to find a new way to say this. It begins to lose its punch after you have heard it so much.

The uniqueness hits you like *American Beauty* because it is not bland. It is dynamic. When you get the uniqueness of being, and you are in the container of a relationship that works, it really makes everything blossom, prosper and come alive for you.

These two actors, the anima and the animus—for all their evil and ugliness—are pushing for that to happen and they are not goody-goodies. They will do whatever it takes to throw you in the soup, to get you into your life. They have not been baptized! They don't operate according to the rules. They don't go according to what "should" happen—that is what is so royally juicy and explicit about Lester's flaming affair with the young cheerleader. It captures in visual imagery the sexuality of the anima for a man. That is where he finds it—*if* he finds it—and if he doesn't, he spends the rest of his life chasing skirts. That is where he finds the energy for his own life—in roses covering a female body, and it is not according to the rules.

I want you to begin to get a feel for where the lovely creature, the anima, is in *your* own life. Likewise, if you are a woman, where is the creature riding on your shoulder, the animus? Where is he pointing his lantern or his finger and what is he doing in your life? We will continue to gather our energies to deal with these characters, and we will work through the American Beauty dream of our own dysfunction in relationships.

Chapter 3

Paying Attention to Ourselves

WE WANT TO CONTINUE our discussion of the two creatures, the anima and the animus—"everybody's favorite couple"—so exemplified by the dysfunctional relationships in *American Beauty*. At the outset we will listen to the march from Verdi's opera, *Nabucco*, so that we can gather our energies to deal with these creatures and have a good spirit about them.

Nabucco is about the defeat and the captivity of the Israelites by Nebuchadnezzar, King of Assyria in Babylon. It is about the faith and courage of the Israelites and their eventual freedom, as Nebuchadnezzar is himself imprisoned and confronts his own faithlessness and evil. My fantasy of this music is that it is a victory march—indeed, it became a national anthem in Italy during the Second World War, marking the defeat of the actual Gestapo. It seems appropriate to our task. If the Israelites—and even Nebuchadnezzar himself—could overcome captivity and imprisonment in the desert, then we can do it also with the negative anima and the negative animus.

Verdi's music has that spirit. It helps to raise the level up a bit for us, to expand our awareness, which is what you need in archetypal psychology. We get so bogged down in our personal issues, that we lose sight of the bigger picture which the objective psyche has to offer. I am very envious of Verdi. He lived and wrote most of his music in the 1800's, in a different age. One can hear in his music that he had a happy soul; throughout the opera, *Nabucco* has one aria after another. Recently, we went to see *Nabucco* performed in Houston, followed the next evening by a twentieth century opera, *Cold Sassy Tree*. What a contrast. There was not a single aria in the modern work—it was dark, heavy, and atonal. These are the times we live in. They are not happy, and they are askew. *American Beauty* certainly touches into that problem of our time.

Last chapter we had roses for our lecture, here we have zinnias. Zinnias are the flowers of the sun, and have an Aztec heritage. The summer is the high point of the sun in our hemisphere, the zenith of masculine energy, and it also happens to be in the astrological house of Cancer, the sign of the family. Cancer also happens to be emotional and a little unstable, as a water sign. So, it is an appropriate time for readings on the anima and the animus. Working on this material, I get to do my own personal work as well, working things through in my own relationships. That is what it means to be in a relationship—to work things through.

On Father's Day, I read a wonderful article, "My Father's Troubles," a memoir of love and madness, about a man whose father suffered from mental illness and the difficulties he endured, but also about the love that managed to come through. He wrote, "When I look at the old snapshots, I am always surprised at how happy my father seems." Well, I don't know if you remember, but there was a similar scene in the movie. Lester was looking back at his life and at the picture of Carolyn and his daughter, and he was saying "how happy we had been." A shocking and striking contrast to where they were now.

It has been said that women talk too much about relationships and men don't talk enough. Welcome to the middle ground. The magazines today are chock full of stories, and now, on the internet—"X seeks Y.com"—the online relationship network has arrived. So *American Beauty* can be solved. Let's see—envy, pride, lust, jealousy, hope, and disappointment—it's all there. What else is going on in your relationship? You can chat with people who have been there, who are there, or who will be there (sooner or later). I found it amusing. Let me tell you about this cartoon: this gal is obviously passionate about the guy sitting there on the couch with her, and she is saying to him: "I want to get married and start a family with you, although only God knows whom I want to finish it with." And therein lies today's tale.

Today's problem is that we are not living in the "good old days." It is the difference between *Nabucco* and *Cold Sassy Tree*—the difference between consciousness and unconsciousness. Too much consciousness does not bring bliss, it does not always produce a happy tale. When we see two young people blissfully going off into the sunset today, we give

Zinnias

them our blessing and say, "I hope they don't wake up too soon." The bliss that they feel will get them into the soup soon enough.

The movie *American Beauty* comments on what is wrong with the American family. By viewing and commenting on "the appearance of things on the surface"—symbolized by Carolyn's roses, her white picket fence and her happy pleasant dinner music—and then showing what happens when the real substance is ignored, things go terribly wrong, and there is a terrific sense of irony. As both von Franz and Edinger have said, "Movies are very much like modern dreams, or the fairy tales of a culture," especially when they create so much resonance. *American Beauty* has that quality.

The chances are—if you go to see movies—your complexes will get hit and you will have a strong reaction. For a lot of people, *American Beauty* was not a very happy or a pleasant movie. Many people told me that they walked out. Many others didn't like it at all. When that happens, there is a strong chance that your complexes have been whacked. So, what do you do when that happens? If you are able, it is always a positive thing to be able to stand the tension and take it. Try not to walk out, or run away. Then, if you are able, try to reflect on "what drove me crazy" in this movie, or in that scene, or in that book. You need to pay attention, because that is where you find your psyche. There is your answer: the way to find your soul is in your reactions. I think that is important enough to repeat. *The way to find your soul is in your reactions.* (cf: Edinger: *The Psyche on Stage*)

It is hard to see our own resistances, but when we look at them at face value—even though they may be hard to take—we can begin to see them archetypally, and then they can be very instructive and helpful. But first we have to calm the "five-alarm" fire engine response enough to be able to take a look. Or, if you don't mind a little Tabasco in the fire engine, then just bounce off the wall and say, "This thing is driving me crazy and I just need to express it!" But the important thing is to feel it and own it, even if it is a perversion, even if it seems to be the most perverse thing you can possibly imagine.

It is important to accept that we all have our perversions, and the role of the exterminator is to "fumigate them." But consciousness demands that we not push them down or ignore them or repress them and pretend they don't exist. The way to find the psyche—your soul—is to pay attention to the processes that go on.

Jung mentions several ways that we can do that, ways that—more often than not—we overlook or ignore:

1. *Not-consciously recognized personal motives.*
   How do we recognize them? Through your dreams. Through your projections. Through a complex.
2. *Overlooked meaning of daily situations.*
   How can we get the meaning if we overlook them? They are like little gnats. They don't go away. Ask yourself, "Why am I still remembering that?" "Why is that still bugging me?" I overlooked it—"personally, it didn't seem to be important, but something in me is not letting it go away." Acknowledge that— Jung says that the meaning of these daily situations we overlook are the conclusions we have failed to draw. Then you come to a lecture and hear this brilliant exposition and you realize what you should have concluded. Life will bring a platter to your table, a platter full of great food, but only if you are interested in nourishment. You have to be interested.
3. *Affects we have not permitted ourselves.*
   Affects mean our strong reactions. Those are important. Our inner raising has told us that we should not react that way, feel that way, or think that way. A good example of that may be found in the opening scenes of *American Beauty*, when we are shown Lester's masturbation. That is a barely permitted or encouraged point of view.
4. *Criticisms we have spared ourselves.*
   Another important one. Jung says, "The more we become conscious of ourselves through self-knowledge, then act accordingly, the more of that layer of the personal unconscious will be diminished." Why is that desirable? Because God and life are trying to make bigger people out of us, bigger than little old egocentric nerds. Seen archetypally, *American Beauty* can enlarge us.

All of this requires paying attention to ourselves. I want to begin with some follow-up from last week. I hope you got the image of communication in relationship as being similar to that of a game of catch. The important thing in that game is to keep the ball in play. When we drop the ball, throw the ball away, or when we throw it at the other party, then that is not keeping the ball in play.

The interesting thing is that we all see it in *our friends* when they throw the ball at us. They love to throw it at us, and the only possible reaction we can possibly give is to throw it back at them. I am always astonished by people who have this much insight, but who come across like gangbusters—they evoke this enormous response back at them, and then they are hurt. Well, you have just unchained your gorilla and sent it out on the street, and people are just protecting themselves. Why are you now hurt that they are not embracing you? That is what happens. The more insecure we are, the more likely it is that we will unleash our gorilla instead of just talking—we will throw the ball at the other person, instead of playing catch. We need to play ball.

There are all kinds of scenarios to this imagery, but the point is, we need to keep the energy going, to keep the ball in play. As someone said last week, "What if you are tired of playing?" If you are tired of playing, what does that say? It could say, "This game is not very much fun. I want out." That's a bad sign for the game. But it is important to know where you stand and not to pretend. Lots of us play pretend. We think: "I'm supposed to keep the ball in play. I had better keep talking, and we chatter away." We don't want to admit the game is going nowhere, and we need to face that and say: "This is no fun."

Another question is, "What if they change the rules of the game, and I don't like the game anymore?" Well, one has to protest to the umpire. One has to say, "Wait a minute. This isn't the way we started." That is important to recognize and to say, to get the ball back in play.

The difficult thing for introverts is that their energy tends to go within. Introverts will have a Freudian feast in their journals, while the landscape out there is barren, and no one gets touched. You cannot have an orgasm in your journal. That simply doesn't count. You have to be out there, connecting with people. Of course with the extravert, the opposite problem occurs. The energy goes all out: then what happens is often very confusing, especially when the extrovert is anxious or tense. Then it becomes like diarrhea, in which everything comes out and you don't know what is what anymore. It is helpful to be aware of the differences between those two—the introvert and the extrovert.

In the film, *American Beauty*, the couple is a good example of the introverted husband and the extraverted wife. The introvert tries to keep everything within and not work it out. Or write everything in the journal- that would be enough. Or, like Lester, in masturbation, where he has his fantasy life, but nothing else. He even admits that from the start: masturbation in the shower is the high point of his day. Carolyn is the opposite. Everything is out there—the roses, the sales career, and the facade of wife, career, and mother—all one perfect performance after another. She is trying to create a perfect image, only guessing that what she does is somehow important in the overall scheme of things. A poor substitute for love, isn't it?

◈◈◈◈◈

In *Oprah* magazine recently, Jane Fonda actually apologized for her photo shoot taken in Hanoi, during the Vietnamese war, saying "I hurt so many. It was the most horrible thing I could have possibly done; it was just thoughtless." Then the interview turned to her separation from Ted Turner, and she answered "Ted is a soul-mate. I care about him. He means the world to me, he taught me to be happy." They separated, she said, "because we changed. I changed." (perhaps she caught her animus there and said, "I changed" instead of "we," because she cannot speak for him. When you are the one being interviewed, you speak for yourself.) So, she corrected it to "I changed." Then she added, "Are we happier by ourselves than we were together? Well, that is not clear."

If we were to apply a little of the psychology we have been talking about on that, what would we hear? We would hear, "We both changed," and we would read that to say, "the projections fell away." And guess what the result was? "We saw each other differently."

I don't think they changed. I think they stayed the same. They just saw each other differently, as, of course, projections do fall away in a real relationship. That is the great thing about relationship. It is impossible to keep projections going if you are living with someone closely. Relationships kill the era of the gods and the goddesses; that is why they are so important. Romance, illusions and fantasies belong to the realm of the gods and goddesses. They are *illusions*. If one has to deal with a flesh and blood ordinary human being, then it is impossible to keep those things going. One has to say either "I don't like reality," "I don't like him," "I don't like what this love thing is all about," or "I want out."

The other option is to say, like Robert Johnson does in his challenging book, *We*, "We have all got a romantic love fixation disease." It is the Western world's illusion, *par excellence:* we consider it part of our fate to be riding into the sunset, happily ever after. I hate to tell you, that is not our fate. It cannot be. It won't be. That fixation is an illusion. Anyone who tells you differently is full of it, or living on another planet. Real love is working out the corners and the shapes with another flawed human being, one who is flawed and wounded like you.

As someone said to me today at lunch, "It means ignoring and forgiving a lot of things." So, the projections fell away for Jane and Ted, and as Adolph Gugenbuhl-Craig wrote in his wonderful book, *Marriage— Dead or Alive?*, "Marriage has to be an individuation workshop, or it will be dead." Like in *American Beauty*.

Whether Jane and Ted are happier together or apart is, according to Jane, "not yet clear." You know what I think? I think they aren't happier. In our culture, we don't have much glue to hold relationships together any longer. We did in previous ages when marriage was not only a legal state of being- it was also an "ecclesiastical" one, and woe be unto you if you broke your vows, your commitment.

Now, everyone breaks them, even if the good Catholics, the fundamentalists, and the Republicans who are trying to get back to the "good old days." It doesn't hold. It doesn't work. It now takes voluntary, conscious agreement, and even then you have difficulties. Many difficulties.

Thirty years ago. in her book *The Feminine in Fairy Tales*, Marie-Louise von Franz spoke to one of these changes. She wrote. "Now that the poison of aggression has gotten into women, difficult things happen in women's lives." We must ask, "Where did this poison come from?" It is the aggression of the animus. that is what makes things so difficult. I would go farther. I would add, with a little experience now, that the poison of independence has gotten into women. There has been an *enantiodromia*, a word Jung used, meaning the complete shift from one side to the other. This has brought tremendous challenges.

Women used to be the wife and the mother, and stayed at home "to take care of things"—the home and the children, etc. Now there is great energy and movement toward independence, and in many non-reflective, unconsciously driven women, that gets translated into "I don't want to be tied down." This is especially true in mid-life, when "I don't want to take care of another child" becomes her mantra, and she includes taking care of a man, throwing him into the same basket. Frankly, a lot of men are in that basket because they are undeveloped and because they haven't dealt with their own anima, their own feminine side. They have dumped everything on their women. Women are getting tired of that, en masse, which is healthy. But even though it is a general, collective movement, which can be positive and healthy, individuals can suffer from it.

In the book of *Genesis*, God said, "It is not good for a person to be alone." Having spent a lot of time in both camps, I tend to agree with God. It is not good to be alone. It does not feel good. It is not healthy.

It leads to a great deal of isolation, almost by necessity. So, despite the general movement of change in our time—and the power of the climate which it creates in our modern world—and because of the feeling and woundedness of a lot of women, there arises a considerable inner conflict. As one woman confessed to me, "I want to be married, but I don't want to be tied down."

How can one be both independent and committed? What she left out of the equation—or what her shadow left out of the equation—was that every relationship involves being tied down to some degree. Or as Robert Johnson puts it so eloquently in his book, *She*, "Every relationship involves a death." You can't have it both ways, which is what the shadow wants. The shadow, as defined by Jung, is the thing in us that wants it both ways. The shadow is very popular today. "He" is getting a lot of press. "I want the plusses but I don't want the death. I want the perks, but I don't want to be tied down, I want the security, but I don't want to be bound." But *every* commitment involves a death to something else. That's a fact.

My hunch about Jane and Ted is that they are not really happier apart, but they are too strong for each to stay in the same house. You know what happens when you get two strong, egocentric people together? They blow the roof off.

Notice the language I just used? A big ego does not have to be "strong." A big ego is not egocentric. A big ego is not rigid. It can afford to bend and be flexible. A big ego can afford to be open. Little egos cannot. Little egos are rigid and inflexible. Little egos are defensive. The Self intends us to have big egos, egos that are open and flexible. My hunch is that Jane and Ted are not happier apart. They are only separated, living separately. I think she has unwittingly put into words the modern dilemma. The dilemma is how to have a companion in this "singles" world where the freedoms and the connections of both are respected, and where it does not turn into *American Beauty*. That is the dilemma and that is the task, and von Franz says it can only be worked out one individual relationship at a time. (cf: *"Why There are no Good Men Left–The Romantic Plight of the New Single Woman"* by Barbara Whitehead; 2003)

It can only be worked out in relationship by playing catch and keeping the ball in play. It is essential to know that the negative anima and the negative animus hate each other. They do not *ever* want to play ball. What can we do with these incorrigible creatures?

The fact is that the anima and the animus do not belong out there, in the middle of our relationships. Not Lester's anima, nor Carolyn's animus, not yours, not mine. The anima and the animus do not belong "out there," period. They belong on the inside. Jung says, "They are both mediators of the inner world." That means a man gets to listen to his inner woman, gets to know his inner feminine, gets to fight and argue with her. A woman gets to hear the creature who is on her back, and puts him inside—puts him in a bottle with the cork on it—so that she can hear the one who wants to inspirit her, to give her spirit for her *life*. But if they get between relationships—if they get between you and your wife, your husband, your partner—then it will go wrong because they do not belong there. For example, the strong side of a woman comes out like an armed crusader—aggressively—instead of being inside to strengthen her for her task. Similarly, for a man, his warm side comes out as mushy or sentimental, instead of being inside to warm him and to warm his personality, so that he can be both masculine and related.

The question becomes about my use of the term "big" or "large" to describe the ego, reminding me that Jung said that the ego needed to be small. I want to clarify that. I believe that Jung was using the word "small" in that case as synonymous with "humble," and in the sense of "receptive." And that is important. The ego must remain humble and receptive. The large ego of which I spoke and about which I will talk further is meant as the opposite of the word "petty." To have a large ego means that you are open to the opposite of your type. We are meant to relate to the opposites. "Opposites attract." For example, if you are a *sensate* (a sensation type), in Jung's typology, then you will learn all about intuition by living in relationship with your partner, and you will learn to value it. If you are an intuitive type, you will learn to value sensation, it will make you bigger and more complete. That is where the idea and the feeling and the value of "wholeness" comes from. An ego is enlarged that way.

I also want to clarify another point about the healthy independent woman. What I am addressing is that I have noticed that one of the places a modern woman may find herself stuck is in not wanting to be "tied down" to the exclusion of a close relationship. Naturally, in a woman's individuation journey, there is a push toward independence; that is part of what is necessary for her. But if she gets stuck there, it often turns into a place of bitterness and resentment. That is not where *anybody* belongs. We are talking now about the "stuck" place of women who have become independent and then turn bitter and resentful—in not wanting men—or being angry and resentful at them, or perhaps only wanting men for their money, which is cynical and all too common today. People who remain single out of negation obviously are not healthy.

In dealing with any of these difficulties, and these characters, you must have the courage to pay attention, to listen to "him" in you, if you are a woman, and to listen to "her" in you if you are a man. You need to listen to the voices within. To do that, you have to detach yourself enough from your own background noise to be able to hear what that voice sounds like. Does it sound male? Does it sound female? To really do that as an act of objectivity and detachment, you must dis-identify with your ego enough so that you can hear the voices clearly as separate, or to hear it as the thing that keeps harping on you, pushing you, or scaring you. Fear is often what stops us from listening, or—if we do hear the inner voices- we get scared and get stuck.

In that wonderful magnificent quote from *Symbols of Transformation* (CW 5, p.551), Jung says:

> "The spirit of evil is fear, negation, the adversary who opposes life in its struggle for eternal duration and thwarts every great deed."

If you want to know how to handle your fears, those crazy, irrational places where you are fearful—yes, I'm talking about those "crazy irrational places" where you are fearful, try not to get into denial, resistance, or projection. Try not to get mad at yourself. Instead, ask yourself: "Now what is the one fear that gets me?" When are you most afraid? If you can do that—if you can see your fear—then Jung says that is an evil spirit for you. It is negation. It is the adversary who opposes life; "it thwarts every great deed."

If you want to know how to be a hero, or a heroine, it is simply this— go on anyway. I repeat, *"go on anyway."* And, if you are a damned fool, you will be a damned glorious fool. But you will feel good about yourself, even if you are an ass. I have a feeling that, even if you are an ass, life will come along and correct whatever is upside down. I have my buddy, *Lazarus,* (the sculpture I showed you in the last chapter) to remind me of that, because I see Lazarus as breaking the bonds of fear, breaking the bonds of those complexes which keep us from being fully alive and whole. Those bonds are all the things Jung says "we stuff" (repress, ignore) because we are afraid. The opposite of fear is Life.

Jung says that fear "infuses into the body the poison of weakness and age." How about that? I am quoting Jung here, literally, paragraph 551. "It is he (the spirit of evil), that infuses into the body the poison of weakness and age. He is also the spirit of regression, who threatens us with the bondage to the mother and with dissolution and extinction in the unconscious." Have you heard that voice? The voice that says, "You know, you are nothing. You might as well quit." That is what Jung is talking about—that spirit of negation, which can get really strong sometimes, overwhelming and overpowering. When that happens, that is the spirit of evil Jung is talking about.

What is the solution? What does Jung say? "For the hero, fear is a challenge and a task, because only *boldness* can deliver from fear. And if the risk is not taken, the meaning of life is somehow violated, and the whole future is condemned to hopeless staleness, to a drab grey lit only by will-o-the-wisps."

I was talking to a client who told me a wild, vivid, colorful dream. It was during the Christmas season, and I said, "you can do your dream work at your Christmas party and I want you to check out how many of your social friends look grey, how many of them have been eaten by the spirit of fear." It shows. You can see the difference between "greyness" and "colorful."

Dealing with the animus and anima takes some guts and not giving into fear, and not listening to them. The big message these two negative creatures try to convey is "It's all over. You're not going to do it. You are no good. You are a hopeless case." That archetypal line should tip you off to go to your journal for an orgy of writing with your inner creature.

Relationships have a lot to do with helping us to see more clearly. Marriage today is in a big collective upheaval, which is why there is so much of marriage #1 and marriage #2. One of my male clients put it so eloquently, that what all of his hard work and consciousness had made him realize is that "Our marriage has been really between the animus and the anima. *They* had the relationship. Now that we are clearing through some of the debris, it is amazing to find the real person. But we are just getting there."

Isn't that amazing? The anima and the animus love to keep things going. It is only as we "clear the debris" that we begin to see the other person as they really are, and not as we want them to be, nor as we expect them to be. Just the way they are. Every time that you get upset about the way this person is, you need to ask yourself the great question that Jung asked himself: "Why did I expect her to be any different?" That is what Jung did when he took a woman out to lunch and she disappointed him severely. He said, "Well, why did I expect her to be different?" There he found the anima. So chances are, when our real man or our real woman acts, behaves or lives differently than we want them to be, it is our projection of the royal duo on them that has created the mischief. That is hard to take. It is called "humble pie" and makes for a very small ego in that sense of the word: small, humble and receptive.

Today there is so much longing to find the real father, the real inner father, the one who is spirit and creation for the woman, and for the man as well. Around that father image, there is zest and initiative, risk, and lack of fear, a sense of confidence. A woman left to her own negativity very often can turn very scary and scared, ruled by the spirit of fear. The masculine spirit at its best (without all our projections and biases and resentments) is the one who enables us in the best sense, out there in the world. He is not the spirit of evil. If he has become that for you, that is a negation which needs to be healed.

The sun in summer, the sun in Cancer, is a good time of compassion and empathy. It is so important to be healed of and with your personal father and fatherhood. If you can't find a way to do that, then it is really important that you have a good transference with a positive man to heal the breach within your psyche. In my work I am struck by how many women are still striving, even at age 70, to make peace with their fathers. Something in them knows that this should be resolved—it is so important. How is that done? By the ways we have discussed:
1. Pay attention to your feelings and affects, or the complexes that bring them up.
2. Admit and work with your resentments, disappointments and hurts.
3. Do a lot of active imagination
4. Let them go.

"Letting go" is the best way. A woman with a negative father complex has to be able to get to the place where she is free enough to let all of that go. Whenever the resentments, hurts, and disappointments come up—and they will come up all the time—she can let it go and say, "I am not going to let his bastardom make me a bitch the rest of my life." "It is bad enough there was *he*. Why do I keep it going with *me?*" That is the place where we all have to get to—we have to let the resentments go, in order to be at a new place where the unconscious can lead you.

Have *you* listened to your inner voices? How have they struck you? For example, for the men, what are the different ways you may have noticed the negative anima? Very often it shuts men down where we refuse to talk, often because we *can't*. One place to watch for is the guilt over being quiet and the sense of shame about it, because often that is a very vulnerable place for a man.

Jack Sanford, in his book *The Invisible Partners* says, "the anima in her negative manifestations displays herself in moodiness, sulkiness, pettiness, and in her capacity to poison a man and everyone else around her by creating a bad effect. Negatively, she acts for all the world like an inferior, peevish, overly sensitive woman." That is a good description of a man and the negative anima. He is too sensitive. Everything is touchy and gets to him—that is not a sign of greatness. Men are great artists and creators, but this peevishness is not a sign of greatness. That is a sign of over-sensitivity and the blasted anima, and she needs to be kicked in the butt. Small hurts, when in the hands of the anima, become great tragedies, which she, the anima, feels compelled to avenge. Usually she accomplishes this by making everyone in the vicinity pay. Her weapons are mood, emotionality, poisonous comments and even better, a poisonous "air." So if the anima gets between a man and other people, there is hell to pay. She belongs inside. Otherwise, he begins to get too sensitive, too touchy, too difficult, too complicated, too everything. And, as you may have guessed, the anima evokes the animus. That is when a person needs Verdi.

The animus in a woman is the opposite in his negative form. He is blunt, abrupt, caustic, pronouncing brutal words, which has a certain amount of unpleasant aggressiveness to it. It is as though her masculine side, which properly belongs inside her and lends strength to her character, has gotten outside, between her and other people. That is the wrong place for the animus, just as it is the wrong place for the anima. Mischief, or rather evil, will take over. The fact is, those two are evil. They break up relationships. That is their game.

When a man shuts down, or refuses to talk, eventually he has to rouse himself to save a terrible situation, because he probably knows intellectually that what he is feeling is wrong or inhuman. What makes it worse is that he keeps it inside and the mountain grows larger and larger. Lester's mountain was an avalanche.

The best kind of relationship is when the two people feel safe enough that they can say awful things to each other, not throwing the ball at the other person, but to the other person, saying, "You really disappoint me when you act this way." When you are able to say the thing that you are feeling, then you will find that often—about 99% of the time—you will see that it is an exaggeration. Therein lies the miracle of relatedness. If you have the guts and the willingness, and the "Verdi-ism," to say negative things to your partner, and if you are in a place of trust, then as soon as it comes out, even a moron can see "This is slightly exaggerated." That is the hallmark of both of these nasty creatures—exaggeration. They are the great exaggerators. That is where the poison gets healed. The hurt feelings, the disappointments, the envy, the resentments, all have to be brought up. That is when we separate the heroes and the heroines from the fearful and the grey, the midgets.

Someone recently told me, "I went to an A.A. meeting and when they asked me how I knew I had a problem with alcohol, I answered, 'When I woke up one morning in another state, in bed with two midgets and I didn't know who they were.'" When you wake up with two giants who are making terror of everything and you are near the end of the world with so much exaggeration and mis-exaggeration, then you know you have difficulty with the two creatures. Saying it out loud to your companion, in a good moment, of course, can often miraculously change it. Then you will get out of the clutches of the witch or the sonofabitch. Being in their clutches is what causes 99% of bad moods, depressions, disappointments, resentments, hurts, etc. where our souls get injured by the poisons we keep inside.

In a lecture recently, I said something not quite as diplomatically as I might, and a woman got steamed at me and stormed out. I said, "Oh, my," and went through the list as to what I needed to do. Then I recalled my friend Jack Sanford's words: "Well, of course, it has to be brought up, you know." That is the other part of playing the game of catch—you have to bring things up. *You have to bring the poison up.* Not in your journal. You have to bring it up to the other person. This accounts for 90% of healings in relationships. So I screwed up my courage and gave this woman a call. As it turned out, she "let me have it," but that was O.K. because at least then I knew what the issue was. I no longer had to speculate on it.

I want to close with the exact quote from Dr. Jung which helps so much with attending to our task, and what he called attending to "the unconscious processes that compensate the conscious ego interplay with each other."

> "The ego contains all of those elements that are necessary for the self-regulation of the psyche as a whole. On the personal level, these are the not-consciously recognized personal motives, which appear in dreams; or the meanings of daily situations, which we overlook; or the conclusions we have failed to draw; or affects we have not permitted; or criticisms we have spared ourselves. The more we become conscious of ourselves through this self-knowledge, the more the layer of personal unconsciousness that is

superimposed on the collective unconscious will be diminished."

Paying attention to those things, but saying "I don't know," or "I didn't mean it," will not be playing catch. You have to pay attention to the things you overlook or that you didn't want to see. You have to, and act accordingly—then, as Jung says,

"...the more the layer of personal unconsciousness that is superimposed on the collective unconscious will be diminished."

It is this personal layer that sludges us up, so to speak. To be healthier, that should be removed. He goes on,

"there arises a consciousness which is no longer imprisoned in the petty, oversensitive, personal world of the ego, but participates freely in the wider world of objective interests."

If you want a good description of the small ego in the negative sense, there it is. It is petty, personal, imprisoned and oversensitive. This is what we all have to get over. If you are oversensitive, you are imprisoned there. If you are petty or take things too personally, you are imprisoned there. The wider world of consciousness is the place at which we are aiming. That is our goal. The tough, egotistical bundle of personal wishes, fears, hopes and ambitions, always has to be dealt with by unconscious counter-tendencies. If you are too ambitious, the counter tendency in the unconscious is to be lackadaisical. The psyche is a self-regulating system. If one side is too much this way, the other side has to be that way. If you are too much here, then it will be too much there. It is going to bring that up. It wants to regulate you, and that is why dreams are constantly correcting the ego's position. That is also why many people don't get too wild about their dreams.

A friend (a professional person) called me recently and said, "Richard, we are good friends, but I don't do any of this psychology stuff." Then she said, "I never remember my dreams, but I had this dream twice, the same dream. I dreamed there were chickens running around in my office and making doo-doo all over my desk." She said, "I know that this indicates a serious mental problem, so would you please tell me about it?" We had lunch, and I steered away from giving her a genius solution to her dream, because I knew nothing about her desk, or her life, actually. Anyway, she pressed me and pressed me, and after the fourth glass of iced tea, I said finally, "Do you think you might be 'chicken' about doing something or making a decision?" God! It was as though an electric current shot through her. "I never thought of that." she replied. Obviously, it hit a bone somewhere because since that meeting, she has dramatically changed her life around.

The touchy, egotistical, bundle of personal hopes, wishes and ambitions always has to be compensated or corrected by counter-tendencies. Instead, it is the function of relationship to the world of objects bringing the individual to the absolute binding and indissoluble communion with the world at large. Then you really know you are OK, because you have got that connection and it is not just you anymore. It is the whole planet. That is how archetypal psychology pulls us out of our little chickens, running and making-doo-doo all over the place, and draws us into the victory march of Verdi.

Chapter 4

Defining the Heroic or Redemptive Personality

Before getting started, I want you to look at this tiny etching by Pablo Picasso, called the Black Spider Woman *(page 56, top). Gentlemen—this is what your negative witch looks like. On the other side—the opposite of the witch—is Angela, the seductress, whom we have already met in* American Beauty. *Picasso knew both of them very well. If you don't believe me, read his life story.*

I WANT TO TALK ABOUT JUNG'S DEFINITION of the hero—or the heroine—the heroic quality in the psyche, and how that operates in *American Beauty*. You may remember that my vote of confidence went for Ricky. While I applaud Lester's progress in becoming free and unstuck and well on his way to discovering himself, Ricky is the one whom I have chosen as the redemptive character in the story. Hopefully, you have been doing your homework, and are beginning to listen to your inner voices, as well as the voices of your friends and the tones of voices as you speak with one another in conversation. Our tone of voice speaks volumes about our emotions, about where we are at the moment. Ricky's voice can help us get a good look at what it means to see fear as a challenge. Seeing fear as a challenge is what Jung defines as what it takes to be a hero or heroine.

Here again is the quote from Jung, (CW5, Paragraph 551):

> "The spirit of evil is fear—the adversary who opposes life in its struggle and thwarts every great deed."

"The Black Widow," etching by Pablo Picasso (1953)

Memorize that. Every time I read it, it just blows me away. It is so important. Jung speaks of this as a spirit of negation. The dialogue in *American Beauty* has lots of negation, which I will point out to you so that you will be able to catch it in your daily life. Now one of the greatest riddles to me is why everyone projects out onto others all the capability and skill at our disposal—all the greatness we possess. We see that "he" or "she" is doing a great deed. But it is our own greatness we need to see, our great deed, which gets thwarted. Jung says that it is this spirit of negation, this spirit of fear:

> "Who infuses into the body the poison of weakness and age, through the treacherous bite of the serpent."

Do you see that? The *body* gets it. This spirit of fear is infused into the body, and then we feel fearful, weak, helpless and we are in trouble. This movie carries that theme. Jung says that when this happens, it is terrible psychologically.

> "He is the spirit of regression, of going backwards and giving up."

How can you see this clearly? What are some examples? Suppose you come to a momentous transition in your life, and you have a chance for a big break-through, but you don't do it. Suppose you are faced with a challenge, and you just feel it is overwhelming, and you turn your back. That is the spirit of regression. You can hear yourself say, "This is so hard," "Oh, I am struggling so much," or "Woe is me." Whine, whine, whine. The spirit of evil is fear and whining. It means giving up. Jung describes the seriousness of giving up in the face of hardship:

> "The spirit of evil is fear...who threatens us with bondage to the mother and with disillusionment and extinction in the unconscious."

That is what "bondage to the unconscious mother" means. It means being run by fear. And that leads to extinction. You become just a cipher. You become another face that no one misses because you make no mark on life. To have your own meaning and to carry it to the world is what is really important. To emphasize that, Jung defines the hero:

> "For the hero or the heroine, fear is a challenge and a task."

Fear is a *challenge*. That means taking a work attitude toward your life. It is not about life ministering to you. You have to minister to life. You have a task and creative work to do. It is something very active, as opposed to passive.

I want to clearly distinguish what this means. It means seeing life as a task, as something you must accomplish, bigger even than your job. It is your life task. This does not mean indulging in your pleasures. This does not mean giving in to whatever you like or doing what pleases you. It means something that is a challenge and a task to convey to life. For many people it means doing their "creative writing." Creative because it takes effort; writing, because it means putting something into words, into *outer* reality. And I don't mean in your journal. I mean creative tasks in which you put into words what Jung put into stone at Bollingen. It means putting into words what you have been grappling with during your life, the work that is for the *ages*. Do you know that if you succeed in nailing down the anima or the animus you have done something for the ages? And you need to put it down, so that others can have the description.

Does that sound incomprehensible? Well, first you have to realize that you are not alone in this—you cannot individuate alone, nor is individuation meant just for you. Jung makes that a very important point. We have to convey the meaning of life to others. How do you do that? Not by being a missionary. Not by joining a church and converting people. Certainly not by beating people over the head with your message, or by psychologizing until you are blue in the face. *You do it by doing your own still, quiet work and bringing that out of stone. That gives solidity. Only that.*

So for the hero or the heroine, fear is a challenge and a task, and only boldness can deliver from fear. If the risk is not taken, then the meaning of life is somehow violated. Some of you may recall my previous lecture series on Nicholas Evans' book, *The Loop*. There came the time in the story when Luke had to stand up to his father, Buck, and say "I am out of here. That is enough." It was almost as if everything had been leading up to that moment, and if Luke had not taken the risk, the meaning of his life would be violated. We see moments like that in all of the great literature, and as von Franz said, the great movies also capture the imagination of our time.

In *American Beauty* we have that same kind of heroic moment, when Ricky stands up to the Colonel, and says, "I am out of here. You are fired as my Dad."

Only boldness can work in that moment and all of our lives have those moments. If the risk is not taken, the whole future is condemned to hopeless staleness, to a drab grey, "lit only" as Jung says, "by will-o-the wisp," those fantasies of "if only" and "what might have been." That is the greyness of life for all the people who have missed the chance. They live in the past; nostalgia and sentiment is their daily diet; grey is their color.

❧❧❧❧❧❧❧❧❧❧

That is the introduction to the heroic or redemptive character as Jung describes it, and as we will discover in Ricky. Before we go on, it would be good to listen to another selection from Verdi's *Nabucco* to provide some inspiration This is the great chorus, *Va Pensiero:* The Lament of the Fearful Soul. It could be translated "Give us hope, Lord, God above Help us to face our challenge." Nebuchadnezzar, King of Assyria, has imprisoned the Israelites. The modern stage setting in Houston recently looked as if it could have easily been Dachau or Auschwitz. The Israelites are singing this hymn of hope at the bleakest time in their lives. That is their challenge. It becomes our challenge, too, when we feel imprisoned by overwhelming forces.

I have often talked about astrological Mercury, and what happens when it goes retrograde—the incredible turns of events and *snafus*, which are characteristic of retrograde Mercury may be exemplified in this opera. The King, Nebuchadnezzar, is very inflated and stands up against all the Israelites, saying "No one is going to make me bow to this stupid God of yours." By the end of the opera, he is begging for mercy on his knees. He has been totally transformed, and he is a lot more appealing. Frankly, we are a "pill" when we are doing well, because we get full of ourselves. That is why all good Jungians have learned to say "knock on wood" when we are feeling good about things, because Nemesis, the goddess who simply does not like humans to do well, will come and upset our apple cart. If you think that is superstition, try it sometime. It is the recognition that the psyche is a self-regulating system.

Many people say: "I don't do therapy;" I don't want any psychology stuff." That probably won't work today. Why? Because we now live in the much-vaunted "Age of Aquarius," and being an Aquarian myself, I have some familiarity with the subject. Back to Aquarius, where we now live. The symbol-sign of Aquarius, is the water-bearer. Symbolically, that would mean carrying one's own unconscious (the water). *Today, I think that carrying the burden of one's own water, of one's own consciousness, is the task of our age.* Therefore, one cannot get away with "I don't like psychology," because psychology is the study of the psyche, the study of the individual, the study of the water-bearer. Avoid it then, at your own peril. There is an old saying: "A wise man knows the signs of the times." The sign of our time is Aquarius, the new Aeon, according to Jung. That would be "listening to the stars" in the best sense.

I know that many of you are not interested in astrology, but I want to point out that there are two other important planets, Jupiter and Saturn, which are in conjunction for the next decade and can be very important psychologically. "In conjunction" means that they are having a battle in the heavens, and a tug of war in your psyche.

Why do I keep referring to astrology anyway? In this very scientific, technological age, is not astrology a "bunch of weird stuff," as the kids would say? No, and let us understand why. Jung points out that astrology is an ancient system of "calculating the stars," of seeing and understanding our projections on the various stars, and theirs upon us. Simply put, astrology is a system that can tell us symbolically (vs. predicting the future) what is important "in the skies," now. It affects us. Give it a test in the broadest sense and see if it does or not. And I do not mean some generic hodge-podge "about you" in the daily paper or magazine.

Saturn is about budgeting and being strict and taking charge, making sure you have money in the bank and following the rules. Jupiter says, "What the hell? Let's party! Let's spend." He is on the manic side of the gods. You may notice this going on in your own household. You could say that Jupiter and Saturn are the manic-depressive duo, because Saturn is depressive, critical, the task master, duty-bound, and responsible. Saturn sits on everyone's shoulder and especially among women—he is the archetypal negative father. On the other side is Jupiter, the god of largesse, loveliness, kindness, generosity and support—he is the archetypal positive father. But right now, they are at odds, mainly over money. So if you are concerned with bills and finances more than usual, you can attribute that to them. If you are not aware of such things, then little Mr. or Mrs. Ego gets to be the play ball between these two, back and forth. One day you feel prosperous and the next day broke. If you have some self-awareness, you wonder, "What's going on?" Suffice it to say that when these two are at odds in the heavens, they are sitting right on top of us psychologically as well.

Jupiter, the god of largesse, enters Gemini, and one of the twins likes things fast and speedy (drugs, alcohol, speed, whatever speeds you up). If you relate to it positively, then it is about communication, clarity and understanding. It is about American Beauty. Many know that *MCI*, *WorldCom* and *Sprint* were having trouble, and you may be too, as the sign of Gemini is about communication, media, travel and your inner journey.

So, now is a good time to take a good look at Ricky, my hero in the film who is really able to see beauty in the world. The title of the film is a take off on the rose, and Carolyn's perfect little rose garden—a sarcastic jab at roses so perfect that they are nauseous. Ricky, on the other hand, walks around carrying his Digi-cam in a pack, and looks strange and spooky—he "looks weird," which is what Angela says of him, pronounced in the name of the American collective, judged from the outside. Gradually, however, as we get closer to him, we will find that he is the one with some real solidity. I hope to show you that in this chapter.

The notion of beauty is central to this movie and is very important psychologically, because it is an essential aspect of the eternal feminine. However, it is often accompanied by—it walks hand in hand with— death. It is no accident that relationship leads to death and re-birth. Relationships always mean going to the mountain of death, because you have to say "no" to a lot of things. In the myth of Psyche and Aphrodite, Aphrodite leads her up to the death mountain. I encourage you to read Robert Johnson's exploration of that theme in his book, *She*.

Where there is real relationship, it involves commitment, and where there is a choice, every choice means "no" to other choices. That is where the notion of loyalty comes in. A partner has to be able to expect loyalty from the other partner. For example, a loyal partner should no longer keep looking at everyone else. Very often, this is what makes modern relationships so treacherous. The "demon" convinces them that loyalty, stability, and commitment are old-fashioned—that these traits do not matter. So much of that is "in the air;" it challenges everyone's sense of solidity and what we can base trust upon. "Old-fashioned", "out-of-date", and "not modern" are some of the phrases we use to throw out very important values.

When I wrote last time about that and used the phrase "the poison of independence in women," (quoting Marie Louise von Franz, actually), a number of people got thrown by the phrase, unable to understand what I meant in context. Please note: *all of my work is about giving independence to women.* Many women wake up after being doormats and being submissive all of their lives. All of a sudden they want to "do their thing." Without the self-regulation of their dreams and their psyche, they go the other way. That is par for the course, because after you wake up from something, your tendency is to flip into the opposite, an *enantiodromia*.

The goal, however, is a more mature solid ego which will learn how not to do the Saturn-Jupiter dance, but to hold the tension of the opposites. The manic-depressive person is a perfect example of a person with a very weak ego—the manic-depressive cannot hold the tension. The ego is not strong enough. When you first begin this Jungian work, your ego is not strong and solid and deep enough, either. Strength and solidity of the ego is what this work hopefully enables and produces in you, over time.

I was saying that relationship includes beauty and death, and "being tied down." Ricky is very interested in seeing things as they are, as beautiful, and he walks around with his video camera, focusing on Jane, the pretty girl next door. At first, you wonder about Ricky. Who is this strange character? A voyeur? A pervert? Jane and Angela—in their teenage talk—blast him for filming Jane before she even knows him, and they say he looks creepy. The writers' script, however, offers a different assessment. It reads, "His eyes look much older." The script shows the writer's intent, that Ricky sees things that others do not see.

Hopefully, the actor was able to convey some of that to the audience.

The script has another note about Ricky on page 11: "Beneath his Zen-like tranquillity lurks something wounded and dangerous." So, at this point in the beginning of the film, Ricky looks like the archetypically troubled teenager—isolated, cut-off. There he is, looking standoffish, filming everybody and stalking Jane in a creepy way. He is somber, isolated, taciturn, and looks like everything negative about adolescence. Ricky carries all of that. As if that weren't enough, he is carrying everything negative about being an introvert, which is the "rub" in the film. He is everything our culture does not admire.

His video-cam is focused on Jane, and Jane has to run into the house to avoid his lens. Jane and Angela talk (their teenage dialogue is priceless!), and then the Colonel pulls up in his car with Ricky, to whom the Colonel has just been giving hell about "the fags" in the neighborhood. Jane spots Ricky next door and says,

> "Oh, my God, that's the pervert who filmed me last night."
>
> Angela replies, "Him? No way. He's a total lunatic."
>
> Jane is amazed. "You know him?"
>
> Angela: "Yeah. We were on the same lunch shift when I was in the ninth grade and he would always say the most random, weird things. Then one day he was, like, gone. And then Connie told me his parents had put him in a mental institution."
>
> Jane: "Why? What did he do?"
>
> Angela: "What do you mean?"
>
> Jane: "Well, they can't put you away just for saying weird things!"
>
> Angela stares at Jane. Then her mouth widens into a sexy little smile and she says, "Oh you like him, huh? You are defending him! You like him! You want to have ten thousand of his babies!"
>
> Jane: "Oh, shut up."

Suddenly, Ricky is standing in front of her and a transcending moment in the film occurs:

> "Hi," Ricky says, "my name is Ricky and I just moved next door to you."
>
> Jane: "I know. I kind of remember this really creepy incident when you were filming me last night."
>
> Ricky: "I didn't mean to scare you. I just think you are interesting."
>
> Angela shoots a wide-eyed look at Jane, who ignores it.

Jane: "Thanks, but I really don't need to have some psycho obsessing about me now."

Talk about slicing the guy and raking him over the ground. How's that for a little teenybopper? (Thank God here for Ricky's "strength." Such a slicing remark would have stopped a lot of guys cold!)

Ricky: "I'm not obsessing. I'm just curious."
He looks at her intently, his eyes searching hers. Jane is unnerved by his interest and has to look away. Ricky smiles and walks off.

If you want an instant course in the image of the game of catch that we have been discussing, Ricky has just hit a home run. Why? She blasted the hell out of him with her animus and he took it. He took it—he didn't throw the ball back at her as he had every right to do. He answered her, "I'm not obsessing. I just find you interesting." That is related talk. When one cuts through all the emotionality and the ugly "twins" (the anima and the animus), and gives it back factually without all the dripping tones of sarcasm, knife turning, cutting, or innuendoes, that is related. If you see the whole movie, you will see that Ricky does this throughout the whole movie. Even when his father is beating the hell out of him, he stands right there and takes it—he doesn't give in to rage and resentment—and he answers him factually and relatedly. Related talking and communication means to be able to throw the ball back and to keep the energy in play. "I am interested in you, Jane. I'm not obsessing." That blows her out of the water, and she gets it. That takes a hell of a lot of ego strength. Then he smiles and walks off. I don't know many eighteen year olds who could do that in real life.

But now listen to Miss Collective, Angela:
"What a freak. Why does he dress like a Bible salesman?" She couldn't attack his speech, so she went for the sidewinder.
Jane: "He is, like, so confident. That can't be real."
Angela: "I don't believe him. I mean, he didn't, like, even look at me, once."

Ricky has hit a home run. They simply don't know what to make of him. He hits a home run because he ignores the collective Angela, knocks the animus aside and connects to Jane factually. He deflects all the poison about being a psycho and obsessing about her. *When somebody takes the ball and throws it as hard as they can into the softest spot in you, it is very hard to catch it like he does and give it back.* That usually takes years and years of work with the two negative, sarcastic ones—the animus and the anima.

Listen carefully to the put-down talk. Jane literally hurls the ball at him. She, her devil animus, and Hollywood too, gang up and say to him, "I don't need some psycho obsessing about me." This is what the devil animus can do with psychology. Do you see that? Do you hear what Miss Charming voice of the collective does with psychology there? Psychology is turned into hell. That is a very important thing to know about these two archetypes—the negative anima and the negative animus—in people. They take something that could be very constructive, very helpful, very educational, and then, with their poison, totally transform it into an agent of fear. Then the person hurling such poisonous barbs becomes an agent of evil.

All of us experience that all of the time. It is not just about Ricky and Jane. The negative anima and the negative animus twist things; distort even the most helpful things into accusations and agents of fear. So our task is to learn how to take the awful things that others say and not give them back on the same level.

The script reads: He looks at her intently, his eyes searching hers. She is so unnerved she has to look away. For me that was the opening salvo that alerted me to something special about Ricky—that he was not just any old neighbor. From that moment on, one could say, he is revealed in the film as the "special one," the outsider. Many of us are the alienated ones, many of us come from that place, and so we need to know that archetype. The outsider is the alienated one, the one who doesn't fit in, and the one who doesn't measure up. Ricky carries them all. He carries the American shadow of the misfit in the movie. He even carries Hermes, because he is the one who sees. The whole film begins to revolve around his video camera, what Ricky sees. By the time he gives his great speech to Jane about the beauty he sees in the world, something wonderful happens. She acknowledges him. He is the one who knows. He is not a weirdo.

Angela, on the other hand, becomes the spokesperson for the collective in America and everything that is wrong with it especially the American feminine shadow—the body and how it looks. Ricky carries the male shadow, that is, he is regarded with suspicion and carries all that is unrecognized and alien—accused of being a freak, a weirdo. Angela *becomes* the America feminine shadow—the sexual cravings, the lies, and the deceit of women. Ricky dismisses her—does not even look at her, not once. He finds no beauty or fascination there.

Then the film gives us the personal close-ups between Ricky and his father, the Marine Colonel, who beats the hell out of him periodically, and has an agenda for his son as an outstanding, acceptable young man, with a decent job, with a decent income, and giving off the right vibes, the "right stuff." It doesn't take long to see that he, the father, is carrying an enormous secret, which is corroding his insides. Here is the scene in the Fitts house, when the Colonel and his wife, Barbara, are watching TV like zombies, and Ricky is there, sitting in the middle, between them:

> His mother says to Ricky: "What did you say, son?"
> Ricky: "Mom, I didn't say anything."

That's the way things are at their house. Nothing connects. And yet Ricky, a kid in the middle of that family, is able to carry something. We saw that in the earlier scene in the car, when his father is fuming over the gay men:

> Father: "How come these faggots always have to rub it in your face?"
> Ricky: "Well that's the whole thing, Dad. They don't feel like it's anything to be ashamed of."

Again, notice how Ricky threw the ball back. The father threw a grenade at Ricky's face.

> Father: "Well, it is!"
> Ricky: (knows it's heating up) "Yeah, you're right."
> Colonel: (Eyes flashing, on to Ricky's game) "Don't placate me like I am your mother, boy!" (alluding to his wife, whom he has already wiped out.)
> Ricky sighs. He looks at his father, and delivers that ironic great line: "Forgive me sir, for speaking so bluntly, but those fags make me want to puke my fucking guts out."

Believe it or not, *that* is playing ball. He gave it back to his father, taking literally the wiliness of Jesus' saying, "be you wise as a serpent," because one doesn't argue with the Colonel.

> Father: "Me too, son, me too."

But the script says that the father is taken aback, and then quickly recovers. In the meantime, Ricky is writing his income down in his notebook—$24,000 from his sale of drugs. This is the red herring about Ricky that got a lot of people going about him—he was a "drug pusher." That is even more grist for the mill—when something about somebody really gets you going and you are ready to write him or her off just like that. Chances are, there is a projection of yours at work. Watch out, or you may be missing a hero in disguise.

The next big scene is at the party where Lester decides that he has had it with Carolyn, with his job, with everything, so he is at the party getting drunk. Then he meets Ricky outside near the dumpster, where Ricky is "working" the party. Ricky introduces himself to Lester as the kid next door, and Lester says, "Oh, fine. Glad to meet you," wondering what in the hell does this kid want? Notice what happens. This is right out of Jung's paragraph on Fear.

Ricky and Lester are standing over next to the dumpster behind the service entrance smoking a joint:
   Lester: "Did you ever see that movie where the body is walking around, holding its own head?"
   Ricky: "Oh, The *Re-Animator*." (He's seen it.)

The service door opens and the large catering boss and the sous-chef are peering at them. Ricky hides the joint and the catering boss launches in:
   Boss: "Hey, I'm not paying you—(eyeing Lester suspiciously)—to do whatever it is you are doing out here."
   Ricky: "Fine. Don't pay me."
   Boss: "Excuse me?"
   Ricky: "I quit, so you don't have to pay me now. Now leave me alone."

The catering boss goes inside, mumbling "asshole." Lester looks at Ricky, who shrugs.
   Lester: "I think you just became my personal hero. Doesn't that make you nervous, just quitting your job like that?"
   Ricky: "Oh, I just do this gig as a cover. I have other sources of income. But my Dad interferes less in my life when I pretend to be an upstanding young citizen with a respectable job."

There. He puts it right where it belongs. This is exactly the cross of the strange kid: "how to fit in and look respectable." Ricky pulls it off with panache.

It is also the parents' dilemma. What to do with a strange kid? Do you beat him? Will that make him respectable? Do you play the Colonel and beat the hell out of him and make him have urine checks every six weeks?

To see the conflict in that way is terrific insight for such a young man. Suddenly, from now until the end of the movie, Ricky becomes the teacher. He becomes the teacher for Jane and for Lester. He is the one who has insight.

That is what consciousness does. It gives you insight beyond the collective point of view. When you work with your ego state, it pops out of the collective. Most of us fearfully resist that. We don't want to go there, because it is so lonely and we don't want to be called weird, like Ricky. Angela becomes the voice of that collective, calling Ricky weird and a mental case, remember? The fearful one asks, "Who wants that?" She was the spokeswoman for "everybody out there." She is not just a crazy little teenager; she is a spokeswoman for what you get when you "bounce out," when you are not "in." Hers is the voice most of us resist terribly and what comes right to the heart of FEAR. Some of us don't even have a problem about being discovered, we were born weird. We are already "out." Therefore, the task is to learn how to take it and to be savvy, like Ricky. We have to learn how to give it back and not be bullied by the bosses and the bullies of the world. We have to be able to throw the ball back. But you must not do it on their level. You must do it on a related level; that is the task and the trick.

The fear of not being with it, of not being in, is most aptly expressed by Angela. When she talks about being the sexual kitten of the school, the one desired by everybody, she admits her greatest fear: "Otherwise, I would be ordinary. And there is nothing worse in life than being ordinary." The truth is, the willingness to be ordinary is a great faculty, because it is beyond the collective, the tripe, the repeated clichés, and all the stuff that people are "supposed to do," which blocks uniqueness and individuality and individuation. For illustration, Marie Louise von Franz tells the story of the man who saw Jung in his casual clothes at play down by the lake, and said, "Isn't that the famous Dr. Jung?" When Dr. von Franz replied that it was, he was amazed, saying, "You'd never know it to see him like that!" (Film: *Remembering Jung* with Marie-Louise von Franz).

Angela has suggested a way for Lester not to be "ordinary." Lester has overheard her tell Jane, "If your Dad worked out, I bet he would be really hot," meaning sexually. Ricky is videotaping, while Lester is now fanatically working out, hoping, of course, that this is the way to bring reality to the lovely rose petal fantasies he has been having about Angela. Ricky entertains no illusions. He cuts right through them. For example, earlier, Ricky had told Lester about how his Dad, the Colonel, wanted him to be a self-respecting young man, and somehow believes that Ricky is earning enough for all of his camera equipment through his catering jobs, not selling drugs.

Ricky then comes out with the wonderful insight:
"Never underestimate the power of denial."
Meaning: even the Colonel can refuse to face the likelihood of Ricky selling drugs. Or, of Lester realizing that Angela is only a teenager.
Lester smiles, and says, "This kid is cool!"

In another scene, this one between Jane and Ricky—and Angela, of course, playing the shadow—Jane and Angela come upon Ricky filming a dead bird. We get the first glimpse of Ricky's interpretation of beauty for what it really is. This is just after the scene of Carolyn and Buddy (the real estate king) going at it in the motel room—the other relationship going on in the film—providing at sharp contrast to Ricky's viewpoint. There he is with his Digi-Cam, a dead bird lying on the ground, decomposing.
Angela says, "What are you doing, Creep-o?" as only a teenager can say it. The camera faces them.
Ricky replies, "I am filming a dead bird."

There he is again, consistent. He just gives the answer back. No sarcasm. No anger—he is filming a dead bird. They keep trying to get a rise out of him, jabbing at him, especially Angela.
Angela: "Why?"
Ricky: "Because it is beautiful."
Angela looks at Jane, and tries not to laugh. "I think maybe you forgot your medication today, mental boy."
Ricky: (Ignoring her comment) "Hi, Jane."
Jane: (Uncomfortable at this point at his filming her) "All right, now, I want you to stop filming me."

At this point you expect that Ricky might be so invested in his camera, and really so intent on her, that he will not stop. Finally Jane has the related courage to bring up the issue about his filming her, and you expect him to argue, to get upset, or to say, "Oh, you don't understand." Instead he says: "O.K."

If you are not convinced by now that Ricky has got something, this ought to convince you. He simply says "O.K." He looks at her curiously, his eyes searching her, and Angela is totally blown away. She begins to storm off. Jane, however, does not follow her lead.

> Jane: "Hey, you need a ride?"
> Angela, the "American" spokeswoman says, "Are you crazy? I don't want to end up hacked to pieces in a dumpster somewhere. Do you?" That is what "America" thinks of weirdos.
> Ricky: "It's O.K. I'll walk. But thanks."
> Angela: "See. He doesn't want to go anywhere. Come on, Let's go."

Angela starts off, Jane stays; Ricky smiles at her and she almost smiles back, but then she says to Angela, "I think I'm going to walk, too."

Angela stops and stares. She knows now that she is losing Jane to this creep. She has all this power, and she is losing her best friend. She doesn't understand it, because this is not what life is supposed to be about. It is supposed to be about being sexy and being pretty, and being a star, desired by every boy in school.

> Angela: "What? Jane! That is almost a mile away and you are going to walk, with that creep?"
> Jane: "Yes."
> *End of scene.*

That was homerun number two for Ricky, as far as I am concerned. When Angela, the witchy voice of the collective, trying not to laugh, says, "I think you forgot your medication today, mental boy." he turns to Jane and says coolly, calmly, "Hi, Jane." He's impressed me.

I think, "Damn. I wish I could do that." When Jane asks him to stop filming her, he doesn't argue. He doesn't try to explain. He doesn't try to rationalize. He doesn't deny it. He doesn't do anything defensive. He is not self-conscious. He just says, "O.K." If that is what you want, "O.K. I'll stop."

This is called *relatedness of the maximum kind*. On the opposite side of this dialogue, where there are Angela's vicious, slashing comments, I hear a lot of the archetypes rampant today in a violent, vicious, slashing society of words, in which young people talk like that—"I think you forgot your medication today, mental boy." Jung has a wonderful essay about words. He says that people today do not realize the importance that words carry in communication. The importance of words, in what we say and how we use them can come back to haunt us.

There is a great story of the penitent who went to confession about lying. The priest told her to take a pillow to the top of the cathedral and rip the pillow, which was filled with feathers, and let the wind take the feathers. Then he said, "Your penance now, is to pick up all the feathers." "That's impossible!" she cried. The priest replied, "That is exactly what your tongue has done."

Our words are very important and Ricky just cuts right through all of the emotionality in such a wonderful way, without condescension or sarcasm, just very connected and very related. Connectedness and relatedness mean answering back, talking to the point, not about bringing up side issues or other issues, not getting off on our rage, or tangents. "Hi, Jane"…"I think I'll walk"…"Thanks for the offer."

It takes a lot to be able to do what Ricky does. If you don't believe me, just watch your conversation for one hour in the next week—just one hour. I know many of you are familiar with Irene de Castellejo's wonderful classic, *Knowing Woman*. She has a chapter in her book called "Bridges" which is about communication, and which, I think, is the best of its kind anywhere. It is superb. If you can, read it slowly and carefully, with feeling. She writes from the feeling function. She conveys the importance of speech, especially for the feminine, and she writes something very surprising. She writes that women seem very loquacious, that women are noted for being full of words, but that women are not really good at words. Guess who is? Mr. Animus—the inferior masculine—is very good at words. In fact, he is never at a loss for words. He has a word for everything. But a woman is so close to her feeling function most of the time, that to put things into words is very difficult. That is what Castellejo sees. It is a great chapter, a masterpiece. I recommend it to you in this context. She gives such feeling for how words may be used to build a bridge between two people.

Ricky carries that archetype for me in the film, as a builder of bridges, even in very crazy situations. Despite Angela's (the collective shadow) mocking and ridicule, he never takes the bait. That is heroic.

It is the hardest thing in the world for a man to do in the presence of the negative animus, not to take the bait. It is the hardest thing for a woman to do in the presence of the negative anima, to not take the bait. To be "cool" is the goal. Not cool as in aloof or distant. Cool in the sense of being connected and related and not to get into the mire. Cool in this sense means being centered. *That* is heroic.

I want to mention one other notation in this scene. As Jane and Ricky are walking home, walking without speaking, he seems comfortable with the silence; she doesn't.
Jane: (finally) "So how do you like your new house?"
Ricky: "Oh, I like it."
Jane: "The people who used to live there fed stray cats so they were always around and it drove my mother nuts and then she cut down their tree."

Then a funeral procession appears. It passes by slowly.
Ricky: "Have you ever known anybody who died?"
Jane: "No, have you?"
Ricky: "No, but I did see this homeless woman who froze to death once, just lying there on the sidewalk. She looked really sad. I got that homeless woman on my camera."
Jane: "Why would you film that?"
Ricky: "Because it was amazing."
He didn't defend it, he didn't explain it, and he answered, "Because it was amazing."
Jane: "What the hell was amazing about it?"

A pause. He thinks, and then replies:
"When you see something like that, it is like God is looking right at you for just a second. And if you are careful, you can look right back."
Jane: "And what do you see, when you see God like that?"
Ricky: "Beauty."

Then there is a scene when he sneaks into his father's gun case and display rack to show Jane the German plate and turns it over—there is a Swastika. Not surprisingly, the Colonel has collected this German Nazi plate. This bums Jane out, and they move on into Ricky's bedroom, where they undress. He asks her, "Would you like to see the most beautiful thing I ever filmed?"

Now you see what has been building up between them—all the bridges being built between them lead up to this moment. It has to build up to trust. Now today, we simply don't know anything about this kind of building up, about communication and being able to share tender, vulnerable moments in this violent culture. You just don't, unless you are prepared to have it ripped apart, or smashed. It has to have build up to share the beauty of all that is behind the moment. Some of us cannot imagine why we have to keep our mouths shut, but Ricky measures life carefully. He has the discipline to contain his mouth. Out of that containment comes the measurement of beauty.

He puts it down on film, he captures it on his camera, and he makes it available for others. In this great scene, they are watching his wide screen TV, and he says:

"We are in an empty parking lot on a cold grey day and something is floating across from us. It is an empty, wrinkled white plastic bag…as the wind carries it in a circle around us, sometimes whipping it about violently or without warning, sending it soaring skyward, letting it float gracefully down to the ground. It was one of those days when it is a minute away from snowing. There is this electricity in the air and you can almost hear it, right? This bag was just…dancing with me like a little kid, begging me to play with it. For fifteen minutes. That's the day I realized that there is this entire life behind things, and this incredibly benevolent force that wanted me to know there was no reason to be afraid. Ever."

You know damned well an ordinary eighteen-year-old kid didn't say that. That is where we started, with Jung, about fear. "That is when I realized there was this entire life behind things, and this incredibly benevolent force wanted me to know that there was nothing for me to be afraid of. Ever." Is that not a wonderful system of belief to have? That is when *American Beauty* reaches toward spirit and transcendence. After all the sex and the mess, the dysfunctional families, the violence and broken relationships and awful words, at this moment it touches into the core of the spiritual life. One could give a lifetime to acquire what Ricky has.

Ricky adds, "Video is a poor excuse, I know, but it helps me to remember...I need to remember.

Jane is now watching *him*, not the screen.......

Ricky: "Sometimes there is so much beauty in the world, I feel like I can't take it...and my heart is going to cave in."

Jane takes his hand and she leans over and kisses him softly on the lips. His eyes scan hers, curious to see how she reacts to what he has told her. One cannot get much more intimate than that.

When we have those moments, we too need a video camera. If you don't carry one around, then you need to carry it in your imagination. You need to record it. You need to play it on your "screen." You need to play it however often it takes, because we all need to remember. It is ultimately what Carl Jung called his "Red Book" or our journal. There is so much to the life of consciousness that needs recording. Remembered. Given form. Made concrete.

There is so much beauty in life. Despite all of the mess, and even droughts that get broken with floods, it's still there. The benevolent force is still there—that force which will give you the solidity to be able to say back, to relate back, to keep the ball of life in play with energy, with grace and with beauty. Ricky is the spokesman for that benevolent force. And because he does speak for that, he is a hero.

Chapter 5

Finding Our Way Through

IN THIS CONCLUDING CHAPTER of this material on *American Beauty*, I want to focus my remarks on the American shadow and the will to power, and how that interferes with finding our way through what seems to us impossible situations, both in the film and in our lives. Before I begin, I would like to call your attention to a recent edition of *Psychological Perspectives* (Number 40, 2000). When I was working up this material, it arrived as a synchronicity in the mail. It contains a very good review of *American Beauty* by Joyce King Heyraud. I don't know her personally, but I found her reflections well done, and basically in agreement with my own.

Those of you who understand my work know that I am one who pays close attention to synchronicity. I believe it is important to notice the things that coalesce at the same time. So, along with the review of *American Beauty* in *Psychological Perspectives*, two new images arrived in the mail from Florence, Italy. We have talked about the sun and its energy, and so here is the first image, the sun. The sun is the symbol of masculine generative procreative power; and you might be interested to know that the sun is also a symbol for the city of Florence, the seat of the Renaissance. This city, which gave birth to so much, and still considered the flowering of Western art and civilization, was empowered by the sun, but with a remarkable connection to the feminine.

The Face of the Sun, Symbol of Florence

Here is the second image from Florence. It is the

image of a man, a man who could be Dante, Michelangelo, Leonardo, Raphael or any of the great men of that great city. You see one man and three women, which makes four, the *quaternio* (the quaternity), the number Jung tells us represents wholeness or completeness. These images suggest that somehow the masculine power in that city was always connected to the feminine. And in no small measure—three to one.

The Renaissance began in Florence, and this image is from the Middle Ages—it captures the feeling of Florence. Now I want to show you some modern images with which to compare it. This magazine-*Esquire*—also came in the mail, and here are the American "girls of summer." We can see that these girls of summer are far away from this image of Florence. We can see that Hugh Hefner's *Playboy*, and the Pure "playboy" spirit, do not a Renaissance make. What we need is a Renaissance, a true flowering of the sun—the masculine creative power—connected to the feminine. That is a wonderful place to begin—for you can see the power of Eros in these images, and you can also see the problem, the disaster we encounter in *American Beauty*.

To review, we have four main characters in the film: Lester and Carolyn, the Colonel (We hear his first name—Frank—only once in the film; even his wife and son call him the Colonel) and his wife, Barbara. The Colonel is so identified with the military and to that kind of patriarchy that he is almost too easy a target, and we never get to know his wife. She has been "wiped out" long ago. These four are stuck in the land of non-Eros, of non-relating. They are not playing catch. Nobody is interested in throwing the ball back, except violently and abusively. Nobody is even interested in the energy that comes from the game of catch. So, with all of our delving into the characters in the film, I want to remind you that the real centerpiece in all of this is Eros and relatedness.

As such, Eros has been the focus of this book. We have talked about the anima and the animus and how those two "creatures" break up the game of catch—you could even say that this film is the archetypal mirror of those two dark characters, the anima and the animus—and how "they" won. Even though there is an alchemical quaternity in the two sets of parents, it is only Ricky who tries, through Eros, to connect to life. Ricky has not lost touch with the sun; he has connection and creative forward energy, despite the violence and the rage of the Colonel. It is also Ricky who tries to kidnap Jane out of that dysfunctional imprisonment and to lead her to a new place.

Florence Renaissance painting

I think Ricky and Jane are metaphors for all of us. None of us is here listening to this because we come from the "All-American Apple Pie" family. All of us come from a dysfunctional woundedness and carry that. So, while it *is* hopeful to talk about Ricky and Jane, we also have to face the fact that they have some long and heavy-duty work ahead of them. They are burdened by all the complexes of these four parents—and that is a lot.

I remind us all to not be too smug. I want you to be "in it"—to feel where it touches you, where your personal connection is. Did you begin to hear the anima or the animus in your tone of voice over these last chapters? Did you notice the power drive in those tones of your voice? I want to stay with that thought, because Jung said, "Where there is love, there is no need for power. Where there is will for power, love cannot exist." (CW.9i)

The Colonel and Carolyn are the two power-driven characters in the film. Barbara and Lester are on the depressive side, that is, they are under Saturn, the "dark negative one" we talked about in the last chapter. They are passive, "run over," rendered dispensable and irrelevant. Barbara barely breathes. Lester is just beginning to awaken from a long sleepwalk. In contrast, Carolyn and the Colonel are going to make this work no matter what. Many of us have a power drive problem. Others do not, but tend to be overrun by those who do. Where does this problem touch your life?

༺༻༺༻༺༻༺༻༺༻

Fritz Kunkel has described the four different types of ego. The *Star* is the type of ego who likes center stage, the achievers who seek to make a "name for themselves." The *Nero* is the type of ego who likes to push others around, bully others, and tyrannize others. The *Clinging Vine* ego tends to cling to others and situations, always complaining or hurt. The *Turtle* ego is the one who hides in a shell. *Turtles* and *Clinging Vines* do not have a power drive problem, but the *Stars* and the *Neroes* do.

Carolyn is a star. She wants to be Queen of Suburbia, Queen of Real Estate. There she is with her perfect garden, her perfect gardening outfit (her perfect clogs, her perfect gardening gloves). That is the problem with Carolyn—everything has to be perfect. Remember the scene when she is frantically vacuuming the house, the house she is "going to sell today." She is going to make a great sale no matter what. So she vacuums it spotless, and then puts back on her perfect outfit—she could be on the cover of a magazine. The tragedy of Carolyn is that she is so bad at it; she is transparent to everyone except herself. You cannot miss spotting her, unless of course, you are "driving a Mack truck" also. Therein lies the tale. We are always the last ones to see our own "stuff."

I want to encourage you to take the time to write about the characters in the film. Which characters do you love the most? Which ones do you love to hate? These are barometers in your psyche. Don't just project onto "them." Do your homework.

The film is about the dark side of Eros. The film is dark and angry and sometimes overly cynical. It shows the whole dark side of Eros, which is about selfishness—"I am out there for me" or "It's all about doing my thing." Unfortunately, that is where a lot of America is. We hear a great deal about power, about personal power, and the object of the quest in life is to succeed no matter what That is the dark side of Eros. It is not about playing catch. Which characters carry that in the film? Those who are power-driven. The Colonel carries it. But it is Carolyn in the film who most carries that American preoccupation blindly. She is "on a roll." She will captivate the real estate guru, they will do a little number together, and she will be up there in the realm of the gods. But look at Carolyn. She is cold, frigid, and always in a perfect pose. She is the archetype of the animus-possessed woman.

What does that mean? What can we say about the "animus-possessed" woman? About the power-driven woman, the woman who is driven? Let's start with the most obvious—Carolyn is no longer interested in playing catch with Lester. That is so obvious, it is ludicrous. She has written him off years ago. Less obvious is that she is no longer interested in playing catch with Jane, her daughter, either. Soon, it becomes clear that she is no longer interested in playing catch with anyone who does not serve her purposes. Isn't that pathetic? She is so driven that she is totally transparent to everyone except to herself.

What is so ironic about Carolyn is that she has taken something so totally feminine, her rose garden, and totally de-feminized it. She has made it into an antiseptic, euphemized rose garden where all the values of the feminine are changed. You see by her outfit that she allows nothing imperfect. Her primness, her proper facade, her proper order. She cannot allow anything out of place.

The Colonel, the personification of the "Nero" ego in the film, similarly has a "macho" problem, where no one is allowed to touch his prized possessions. When you cannot tolerate anything out of place, watch out. It means that someone is gaining on you and His or Her name is God. You can also bank on who is going to win.

Interestingly, Carolyn's place is in the garden. Gardening the earth, growing roses, all of that, is about the feminine. What do we mean when we talk about the feminine? We mean being earthy. We mean being connected. We mean feeling and receptiveness. We mean not only being able to tolerate something out of place, but to revel in it.

≈≈≈≈≈≈≈≈≈

Do you know the great story about St. Catherine of Siena? All the theologians were arguing about what the size of the soul was. Meanwhile a priest went out as a missionary to a foreign land to convert the natives, but because he was almost blind, he baptized a bunch of penguins by mistake. This created a theological problem to say the least, and the debate reached heaven. All the saints, including St. Augustine, St. Peter, and St. Thomas Aquinas, joined in the discussion, and even Plato and Socrates got into the act. "How can we let penguins into heaven?" they pondered, and as men, reached a masculine stalemate. Then St. Peter suggested, "Let's call in a woman." So, St. Catherine of Siena—the great saint of Florence, no less—was called in and told of the problem. She replied, "Well, give them a soul, but just a small penguin-sized soul." That was her solution. The feminine, if she is true to herself, can always find her way through the rules. That is why we often find ourselves in impossible rule-situations in our journeys. Jung reminds us that the feminine is the one who will help us through the seemingly impossible situation; she helps us to find the new way through.

We can see this in family situations as well, in which the Dad is so firm and hard on the kids, expecting so much, and with his firm discipline, but then the Mom comes in and says "Oh, don't take him so seriously." She softens it down. The feminine way is the way through the harshness, through the deliberateness, the straightness, the absolute unbending of the masculine.

If the woman gets into her inferior masculine, gets the negative animus going, she gets to be like an inferior man. Instead of softening down the harshness she becomes pontifical—more relentless, more abrupt, more hard, and more unbending than any man ever dreamt of being. It is off the mark. It is an aberration. She brings nothing to the party that helps, not even herself. Things go really wrong, It is bad for everyone—it is bad for her. That is what Carolyn does in the movie.

She takes a rose garden and turns it into a lab for the *Smithsonian* or for *Home and Garden* magazine. She cannot tolerate anything out of place or anything wild. We learn that she even cut down her neighbor's sycamore tree because it was ruining her lawn. "To hell with the tree!"—that is her attitude. That says mountains about her. If, instead, she could be funky, learn how to get hot and dirty and messy in her garden, and full of dirt, her Rose/Aphrodite nature would paradoxically have a chance.

The Red Rose, the symbol of full-blown mature sexuality and maternal nature, is covered over by her slices and her remarks, her demands for perfection. That is, until it comes to money. Then she heats up over the guru of Real Estate, her affair motivated as much by her competitive ambition as her animus projection. In point of fact, the garden is the last place in the universe where perfection reigns. In fact, God saw to this when he deliberately and maliciously gave us insects to drive us crazy. In Louisiana, we have so many insects, that it is impossible to name them all much less control them. A garden, therefore, ought to be a place where we can go to chill out, to hang out, to be loose, to be messy. Yet when we see all the perfect gardens and lawns in our suburbs, we need to recognize that *American Beauty* exists everywhere, not just in Hollywood.

Carolyn is a satire of American femininity, and the movie satirizes her to the hilt. Her roll in the hay with Buddy, whom she worships in awe, is driven. It is driven by her terrific animus projection onto him—"I'll get this guy…he's valuable…he is what I want to be…he's got the stuff." As Joyce Heyraud puts it in *Psychological Perspectives*, "the deeper essence of the Eros nature of the rose is never constelled." Certainly it isn't in Carolyn, nor in her affair with Buddy. I do think it is constelled a bit inchoately (just beginning) in Lester, especially in the last part of the scene with Angela when he lets her go and can say right after that, "I feel great!" He feels wonderful. Now he knows he is onto something. Something Ricky has that he admires. Something about playing catch. And listen to the tone in his voice, "I'm great!"

The movie provides us with a picture of the way through, a picture of relatedness—a diagram of Eros so to speak—and of playing catch. Last chapter, I said that Ricky was the model of how to do that—a person who could be cool in the midst of war. Those were my words. I said that "the goal is to be cool." Well, I need to clean that up a bit and make myself clear, because after the chapter, I went home and turned on the TV, and there was President Clinton, being "cool." I caught myself, "Oh, my God! If I gave that impression, about what 'cool' means, then it was all wrong. In the midst of a Presidential campaign, nobody 'loses it'— everybody is 'cool.'" That is not what I meant. We do not want to imitate Carolyn. This is not about faked "cool." It is not about pretense or pretending. It is not about holding the tiger in, or the lioness, or the gorilla that wants to attack. It is a centered coolness, where one is contained, where one's gorilla or lioness is contained. Contained and related. That is the goal.

There is a whole chain of container stores which sells every kind of box or can for those who like to keep things in place. The psychological parallel of that, of keeping oneself contained or "cool" does not mean faking it. It involves a great deal of work. What can we do to contain ourselves? Well, you have to work on the two creatures we have been talking about, the anima and the animus. You have to listen to how your anima or animus goes into overdrive when somebody gets in your way. You have to have it out with that in your journal until you can contain it in your "bag," so to speak. You have to hear how your anima wants to slash back, how sarcastic it sounds, and how you get defensive. Or, if you are a woman, you have to hear how your animus gets didactic or pontificates, how you get rigid and "absolute" in your defense. Defensiveness is not being cool.

Even if you can defend yourself in the nicest way, it is not being cool. Feeling types are especially fraudulent when it comes to this. We can be so civilized and pour the nice, sweet syrup of gentility over everything that is not being cool. That is fake. If you are going to be an authentically contained and related person, it will come from your inner center, when you know that you have wrestled down your beasts. Do you know the beasts? (The ones who want to kill this person, and get back at them for hurting you, or disagreeing with you, or disappointing you.) The negative anima and the negative animus always want to get back. They want to get you back, too. The only way to be authentically contained and related is to talk to them, and say, "That is not the way I want to live my life. That is *not* my Eros. Those are not my ethics."

It will not be easy. There is always a lot of justification going on: "But they deserve it. They did wrong. They mistreated me. I need to tell them how I feel because Richard said to bring it up." NO! These two creatures could quote you every lecture and every book to support their side of the argument, but you have to be smart enough and connected enough and feeling enough to see right through that and to know that what we are talking about is playing catch. It is the energy of the Self that matters. Nothing else. Not your ego. Not how you feel. Not what you are getting out of it. Nothing but the Self. I guarantee you that if you honor the Self, it will honor you. Jesus said, "It will come back to you a thousand fold." He said it and He meant it, and He was right, psychologically speaking. Just as those millions of feathers from the top of the cathedral that we were talking about before, come back to haunt you, so does honoring the Self return to you.

In *American Beauty* the diagram of Eros is one-sided. Egocentric. Carolyn and the Colonel are power-driven, and Lester and poor Barbara are on the depressed side, with all the wrong connections. When the masculine goes wrong, the feminine goes wrong. The *I Ching*, the Chinese book of wisdom, puts it wonderfully in talking about the family: "When everyone is in his or her proper place, all of nature flourishes. When anyone is out of his or her place nothing flourishes."

The *I Ching* tells us about what is required for psychic peace, the opposite of what we see in Lester and Carolyn, the Colonel and Barbara. This is in Hexagram #11. It describes the energies and the proper relationship between them. The Receptive, the eternal feminine energy—meaning the one who is open, the one who receives, the one who makes the earth flower—moves downward from above. The Receptive feminine moves downward toward the creative energy, the masculine, which is below. The Creative, the masculine energy, which moves upward, is below because it has taken its place below the feminine.

That already tells you something. It is not the big guy on top with the poor woman beneath, like the relationship between the Colonel and Barbara, but just the opposite. It is not the feminine on top with no masculine energy from below, as with Lester and Carolyn. The archetypal energies, feminine and masculine, behave in this way—the Creative below, the Receptive above—"their influences meet and are in harmony, so that all living things bloom and prosper." This one line says it all. When they are in harmony, everything else is. But when they are not in harmony, when these energies do not meet, as this movie makes grotesquely manifest, nothing flourishes. The only recourse for Jane and Ricky is to get the hell out of there.

The Hexagram for Peace or inter-relatedness, goes on to say: "Peace. The small departs. The great approaches. Great success. This hexagram denotes the time in nature when heaven seems to be on earth. Heaven has placed itself beneath the earth, and so their powers unite—in deep harmony. Then peace and blessing descend upon all living things. In the world of mankind, it is a time of social harmony. Those in high places shall favor the lowly, and the lowly and inferior in their turn, are well disposed toward the highly placed. There is an end to all feuds." That is what the *I Ching* tells us in the Hexagram for Peace. Unfortunately, we are not at that place in America or the world today. There is no peace.

That leads us to the Colonel, the one easiest for us to hate in the film—precisely because he is so obnoxious, so over the top, so disgusting, so violent—until finally at the end, we see what Jung meant about the power of evil in living color. If you want to get really uncomfortable, just imagine what your shadow is like. What are the behaviors you don't confront in yourself? Then think of the Colonel and it will warm your heart. The Colonel shows us what happens. When we don't confront something, when we don't face it, it gets projected outward and we become a living tornado from hell like the Colonel. Those around us generally die. The awful relationship between the Colonel and his wife Barbara—who is totally collapsed into a robotic-grey zombie—gives us a good picture of what happens to the feminine in a world like that. The feminine is lobotomized by that kind of masculinity. That is not what happened in Florence: It is certainly not what the *I Ching* is talking about. One keeps getting the feeling from this man's "vibes" that something scary is going on, seething underneath the surface. And it is. That is the scariness of repressing the shadow. It comes out violently. This movie is so handy. It makes it so easy to hate the Colonel.

What I want us to do is to take him as a metaphor. The Colonel is a metaphor for your shadow. The side you don't like to deal with, the behaviors you just can't stand to own up to in yourself. If you look at it that way, of wanting to avoid it, it becomes evil. That is the paradox, the scariness of it. The more you resist it, the more evil it becomes. In the fight against evil, you become more like that which you fight against. That is why Jung said that modern man's number one problem is dealing with evil. When Jung was talking about evil, he wasn't talking about generic evil. He wasn't talking about the Nazis or the Russians or the Muslims. He was talking about the evil in your psyche and in mine. That is what we need to see in the Colonel. In all of modern literature I have never seen evil, or violence, nor hatred of gays put more starkly, or in living Technicolor than in this movie. It is not surprising to learn that many of the writers and production personnel behind this film were gay, because this film nailed the American masculine shadow in its portrayal of the Colonel.

The power-driven masculine shadow (and the animus in a woman) does not "allow." It cannot allow, and therefore there is no room for the feminine. As a contrast to all of that, we had an experience at this lecture of just the opposite. Just before the gathering, we realized that we had no flowers here and then we did. It just happened.

Many people do not know how to let things happen, how to flow with life and let it lead you, instead of going into automatic drive to do something. The first thing to do is stop. Stop and try to contain all the fragmented pieces that are running around screaming that the sky is falling. *Try to get them together, and say you will hold their hands, and then just sit there with life.*

Many people do not have the ego strength to do that. It takes a lot of strength. You must be patient with yourself and learn how to hold the hands of your fragmented parts, and to be kind to them. Assure them that you will be there for them. Remember what Ricky said in the last chapter, "There is a benevolent force behind everything which wants me to know that I never have to be afraid." So, when do you practice that? When you are *afraid*. Or, to use Jung's magnificent words, *"The truly spiritual person knows that God's hand is behind everything."* Not just the pleasant things or the beautiful moments or the beneficial—not just what appeals to us, but also and especially what doesn't. That is the test. When you are in hell, and you still hold it together, that is when you get an "A." Not when you keep it all together in heaven. And guess what? Until you learn that, life will conspire to bring you more hells until you get it.

The trick is that you are not aiming to get to the place where you have got it together, and then be free to blow it off. No! Everyone says they love the idea of wholeness, but do you know what that really means? It means that I give God *carte blanche* (full permission) to work on all the areas of me that are lopsided, and all of the areas of myself that I don't like, those areas that bug the hell out of me and make me crazy. Wholeness means that my inferior sides are going to get a world-class workout. If you are not ready for that, then say, "screw the process," "I'm out of here." But at least be honest. You have to say "Enough." to that "Clintonesque" mask. You have to stop saying "I'm into wholeness, and individuation. but don't press any of my buttons or you will get it." "Just watch." "My Colonel will give it to you, baby." No, it is those buttons that will get it. The very ones life will conspire to push and push and push until you get it.

Jung said that we become too "one-sided." That means our smart little ego, which Jack Sanford called the great little trickster, the great cheat, can cheat its way out of the greatest physics test ever. It can fake it. By the time we are thirty, the ego knows what its assets are as well as its liabilities, and it *hides* the liabilities. Then comes the Self and guess what? It is now "open season" on your liabilities. It goes after them because it is trying to make you whole, where you wouldn't go, given the choice. You still won't want to volunteer to go on your own—this isn't a voluntary enlistment here. Nobody signs up for this. It will rattle your cages, press your buttons, get after your complexes, and get after your inferior places.

It will say, "Oh, I forgot about your lecture—there aren't any flowers in July." You will have a desert experience and groan. But then look what comes, if you have a Catherine of Siena hanging around, who can make things happen in impossible situations. We end up with flowers in July after all.

It's not the situation that is impossible. As soon as you throw your hands up in the air and your buttons get pressed, then the Self will come after you. You need to have the right attitude, and not play hide-and-seek with the ego and the Self. You need to be ready to cooperate, be ready to change, or you will have some gruesome days. If God has to pull you by the toenails across the desert, He will. So, if you say that you are into Jung, into wholeness, and into individuation, then watch out for your backside. That is where you will have some work to do. In the places where you aren't good—where you aren't very comfortable—where you aren't superior—where you aren't satisfied—where you can't see—where you want answers—where the Colonel goes ballistic and knocks the crap out of Ricky—there is your shadow.

Something scary is going on with the Colonel. He is sitting on a volcano. He is seething. When we sit on our volcano, it becomes evil and fights against us. The Colonel is violent against the enemies of the established order. He is the male version of Carolyn, the Vacuum Cleaner Queen. Both are run by the will to power.

What is the Colonel's shadow? I think it is the great fear of his own tenderness, which is so much a part of the American masculine scene. He cannot allow any softness, or tenderness in himself—his own feminine side—which he then projects onto gays. Gays carry that for him, and he hates them. The hatred is against himself, and his own feminine side—also portrayed as his wife, whom he has psychologically killed and lobotomized. He would kill his own son, too, if Ricky weren't clever enough to prevent it .

Lest we get too smug and think, "Thank God I'm not like the Colonel," we need to ask ourselves, "What is the will to power in me?" We all have it. It's very simple. We have the will to power when we: (1) want (desire); (2) what I want; (3) when I want it. That is the will to power. I want to make it that clear and simple so no one can wiggle out of it. So, I will say it again. The will to power is when I want my way, NOW, and I am going to get it. That is the will to power. Jung says, "where there is the will to power, there is no love."

In Jung's journey, if you will remember from *Memories, Dreams and Reflections*, there was a point very early on where Jung had to confront and kill Siegfried. Siegfried was the hero in the story of Wagner's *Ring* cycle which carried that shadow for Jung—the will to power, and Jung realized he had to kill Siegfried. He had to kill his ambition. If you look at the story of Jung's life, that is central, that is what went down, what he lived from that point. He had a great falling out with Freud, an irreconcilable disagreement, but never will you see a negative word in print about Freud from Jung. That is something you will never see, even when he was egged on or milked about it by the curious interviewer, "Tell us about Freud's dreams." "No," he replied, for "Such things are greater than life and last longer than life." His loyalty to Freud was outstanding, even though they had the break of their lives over it. That is what it means to learn how to see the will to power. For the rest of Jung's life, for all practical purposes, he was shunned and ridiculed, called a "woolly mystic," and was out of the loop in professional European and American psychiatric circles. The shakers and movers were not where Jung was. In effect, the Freudian establishment took over the world. Jung suffered a lonely exile, in the background, but it was his conscious sacrifice. It was a big one, and it has borne incredible fruit since then.

I remember when I was a young man, I asked the *I Ching* what it thought of Freud and Jung. The hexagram read, "the ascendant one (Jung) was coming to inner power with the people." That was not how Freud saw it. Freud saw the conflict in terms of his own psychology, the famous father-son conflict, the Oedipus complex. He saw it as an attempt by Jung to overthrow him. But Jung saw that he had to contain his shadow and his will to power. He saw that he must kill the Siegfried within himself. That is the difference between straining your will power to make something happen, versus allowing life to bring it into flower. I have evidence that Jung was right. I have lived life long enough now to see many strange things come full circle, when "Richard" kept his grimy little paws off of them, or stopped trying to make them come out a certain way. I have seen some incredible things that would blow your minds if I told you their stories.

The will to power is ambition, desire for recognition, wanting to be up front, being a leader, being recognized, having all those qualities of power, money and fame. These desires have touched all of us. It is usually a driven ambition, and it is unrelated because it doesn't matter whom it hurts.

Related ambition, on the other hand, is contained. It has roles and respects its big leader. Respect means to look up to someone and know that you are in a lower place. Just like heaven. When the *I Ching* describes the creative, the heavenly, it is described as placing itself below the earth. The creative then is shown forth as the flowering of all things. Humility is that attitude of respect, no matter what. The Colonel does not have humility nor a sense of humor. When we lose, if we find that we have no sense of humor about the loss, then our Colonel button has been pushed. That is one way to recognize "him" in ourselves. He is rigid to the extreme, very egocentric. All that matters is "I" and "I am the center of the universe." The difference in the game of catch is that the Self is the center of the universe and I am just a little player.

Some ego examples of the will to power might be helpful here. The Star ego might say, "I am going to make that deal, I don't care what rules I have to break." The Clinging Vine, always hurting, might say, "You left me out, you hurt my feelings." Clinging Vine has endless litanies and complaints. The Nero or tyrant—the most "vicious" of the group—might say, "I don't care who it hurts or destroys. If it ruins or even kills someone, that's tough." And the Turtle? Well, the Turtle doesn't usually have this problem, but sometimes just goes into withdrawal to punish "them." "I will make them feel what they did to me." "I just won't talk. I refuse to discuss it. I'll just withdraw and let them see how it feels to be alone."

The Colonel is the Nero ego driven by the will to power. What makes him scary is that you can almost feel the tightly wound strings around him. Did you read the article in the paper about mental breakdowns being very common in America? Well, you are almost waiting for the Colonel's break, because when the ego is that rigid, it usually breaks. The paradox of the strong ego is that when it is strong, it is flexible, just the opposite of what you might think. It can take a lot. It can bend. The Colonel is not flexible. Perhaps you know people like that. You find yourself just waiting for the explosion. They are scary or you feel nervous around them.

Unfortunately, if you are a hysterical extravert, you won't feel that reaction to warn you or clue you into what is going on. Extraverts are so much into other people's soup, they don't get it, and they don't see it. They only feel "strange." That is participation mystique to the extreme. But if you feel that atmosphere around you, and you know that everyone in the group is not all strung together, then it can cause you to be nervous. People like the Colonel are not easy to be around. They are wound tight as a drum. You don't cross their perimeters.

That is what happens when someone is what Jung called "identifying with the unconscious." When one is identifying with the unconscious, it makes one feel extremely self-righteous. You don't have a doubt, when you should have millions. Their judgments pervade the atmosphere, and if you are around, that means that your atmosphere is also pervaded by their judgments. It is important to be able to identify those people in your life and to treat them accordingly. Talk about an exercise in containing yourself. That is to say, don't avoid them or treat them like they have AIDS, but do give them a wide psychological berth, if you are smart. On the other hand, if you are masochistic, invite them to dinner every day and have a blast, because their rage is extremely scary.

The Colonel is all about masculine rage. We have often talked about fathers and sons in my series of lectures over the years, but there are many women who have an unresolved fear of their fathers and of men. They have never worked this "tightness" out, which keeps them wounded and frightened. It can be enormously liberating to see that the tightness and rage is in him. If a woman can get there, she is 90% home free.

I repeat, *the tightness and the rage is in him.* You are not it, and you are not the cause of it. You are not responsible for it. It is not your problem and you didn't do it. The rage is in him and it is his problem.

That is called psychological objectivity, to be able to know where things belong. Some people are very naive about this. They think that it must be a projection to see where things are, to be "critical." No. You have to be able to see a monster when there is a monster, and call a spade a spade. You have to see where the rage is.

When a woman gets possessed, as Carolyn did, she can come off like the Colonel. Her rage is out of control too. Just as it is liberating to see that the masculine rage is in the man, if you are a woman, it is also liberating to see that the rage is in her, if you are a man. You must be able to see where the rage is. If you had a mother like Carolyn, then chances are your mother was not physically abusive. Chances are her abuses were in words. Nothing can be worse than women being abusive through scathing words. And a man, to be a man, must be able to stand up to that, and not get the sword to cut her head off. On the other hand, he must find a way to not stand there and take it like a "wuss" either. He has to make it clear to her that he is offended, and that she is offensive, not contained, and is being disrespectful. But he doesn't cut her head off with his anima and his poison.

If you want to know how your shadow looks, or how you look when you are in your shadow, take a good look at the Colonel and at Carolyn. The scary part is that we might all be like Ricky or Jane, all escapees from a scary place. To deal with that fear, just remember Jung's words about fear. The only way through is to deal with that fear that keeps you stuck.

To deal with that fear, you must be able to see where the rage is. If it is in them—in Dad or Mom or whomever—that is a great step forward to freedom. You won't ever be in prison again. To keep seeing it will gradually weaken the complex. To stand up to the irrational rage of it will free you and make you able to detach from it completely.

I remember Jack Sanford saying to me: "Richard, that woman has a hurricane for you, and you cannot dodge it." Wow. That wasn't what I had planned to be sure. But you have to be able to take it, like a man. And if you are a woman, you have to learn to go through the harshness, and find the feminine solution, like Catherine of Siena.

The day will come when their bad tempers, their moods, their irrationality and busyness, sharpness, and curtness, will no longer get to you. Then you will know you are home. You are home to yourself, where all of us need to get. It is all about finding our way home.

༺ཞ༻ ༺ཞ༻ ༺ཞ༻ ༺ཞ༻ ༺ཞ༻

My work with you is about un-raveling the complexes, and Ricky is the one who shows us the way. He had a hell of a life, where everything about it could have made him bitter, resentful, power mad, and revengeful, but he carried it clear within himself and in a way that did not let the hurt and the woundedness stop him. His forward moving energy kept him moving forward. That is the way to identify your journey. You can tell when you are stuck, trapped, not moving, or being possessed. You can feel it when the Colonel is out with his rage, wherever your rage goes. In just that way, you can find where you are. Ricky escapes from the controlling influences of his father's love—the dark places—and he tries to free Jane from her parents' dark cauldron of indifference. Ricky and Jane are metaphors for all of us, trying to get free. A metaphor for trying to connect.

Their bond is going to be burdened by the inherited malaise of their families and culture—the overwroughtness of the patriarchy (as portrayed in Carolyn and the Colonel), the irresponsibility of the patriarchy (as portrayed in Lester), and the dismal disconnection from the nourishing mother, which is the source of everything that gives life. We all need a place where we connect to the positive mother who nourishes life in us. Ricky and Jane do not have that.

Fairy tales and alchemy tell us about the necessary death of the old king in order for transformation to take place, to happen. Now death has happened to Lester and the Colonel in *American Beauty*. Both have to be left behind if something new is going to happen.

The last scene is of Lester after he is dead. His thoughts of Carolyn and Jane are gone as he realizes his life is now over: "I guess I could be pretty pissed off after what has happened to me. But it is hard to stay mad when there is so much beauty in the world." (There's some of Ricky—Lester caught it). "Sometimes I feel like I am seeing it all at once and it is too much. My heart fills up like a balloon that is about to burst." Now the camera pans as though we are flying over the houses in the neighborhood, and Lester says these great feminine words: "Then I remember to relax. And stop trying to hold on. Then it flows through me like rain. And I can't feel anything but gratitude for every single moment of my stupid little life. But then don't worry, maybe it wasn't so little."

May life flow through you, like rain.

Glossary

Anima
The inner feminine side of a man. An anima possessed man is reduced to that of a second-rate woman; he becomes bitchy, moody, sulky, jealous, possessive and unadjusted. He becomes soft and cannot be counted on. The anima typically comes up for a man in his sexual fantasies (as in the movie) and then is projected on an outer woman. The goal is the anima's transformation from a troublesome adversary into a function of relationship between consciousness and the unconscious. This allows a man access to his own inner riches; he has "soul." He is not trying to find it "out there."

Animus
The inner masculine side of a woman

Negative Animus
The inner man in a woman who is negative; "the man within who wants to fight "every other man." He usually is full of opinions, ideas, generalizations, exaggerations and a prior assumption that are instinctively irritating to real men. "A woman possessed by the animus is always in danger of losing her femininity."—(Jung, CW 7, Par. 337) Eros takes second place to power.

Positive Animus
The inner positive masculine source of creative energy and independence, knowing herself as opposed to "what others think."

Archetype
An inner psychic pattern of the psyche., e.g., mother-archetype, father-archetype.

Eros
In Greek mythology, the personification of love; a force of nature; psychologically, the function of relationship. In women, an expression of their true nature, while for men, it is usually less developed than Logos—thinking.

Logos
The principle of logic and structure, traditionally associated with the spirit, the father world and even the God-image.

"There is no consciousness without discrimination of opposites. This is the paternal principle, the Logos which eternally struggles to extract itself from the primal warmth." —"Psychological Aspects of Mother Archetype," CW 9, Par. 178

Maternal Womb/Mother Complex
Unconsciousness. Whatever keeps us warm and comfy, resistant to the struggles of growth.

Participatio Mystique
(Mystical participation) a low level of consciousness; the classic example of husband and wife "enmeshed" in each other, e.g. the wife finishing the husband's sentence! Identity between a subject and object. Not usually very conscious, so not positive in that sense.

Psyche
A name used for conscious and unconscious psychological processes.

The Self
The inner god-image within the person; the archetype of wholeness; a center beyond the ego. Caution: this is not a benevolent father figure, as in Christianity. It will do anything to achieve the ego's individuation.

The Shadow
The hidden or repressed sides of oneself that one is usually not proud of. The Colonel is a classic example of someone who has repressed his shadow. It can also consist of instincts, abilities and positive moral qualities long buried.

Soul
Best described by Jung as the thing that gives one personality.

About the Author

Richard Chachere was born in Louisiana. After traversing the globe as a young man, he settled in Lafayette, Louisiana, a unique area with a rich melting pot of French and Cajun cultures, and a smattering of Creole and Spanish Catholic traditions. The food is rich and there is music everywhere, spiced by a *joie de vivre* that brings life to even the most dismal swamp.

After high school studies in Illinois, Chachere attended Georgetown University in Washington, D.C. He accessed many seats of political power in the nation's capitol, and he personally met Presidents Kennedy, Johnson, and Nixon. During that time, he also made great use of the rich cultural scene of New York City, especially the art museums, Broadway and the musical theater.

He entered the seminary and studied in Rome, Italy during the four years of the 2nd Vatican Council. He was an eyewitness to history-in-the-making—Pope John XXIII's "aggiornamento," "The opening of the windows"—and to the fall of the Berlin Wall. He later was a personal consultant to Josef Cardinal Suenens in Belgium, traveling extensively with him to many countries.

In 1978 Chachere began his practice in Jungian-oriented therapy, following his own work with John Sanford, Helen Luke and Morton Kelsey. Shortly thereafter, he founded The Acadiana Friends of Jung, a lively center of analytical work and friendship where individuals go to find their own introverted centers. He has lectured extensively since that time and the themes of this work will soon find their way into print. His Opus II, *Legends of the Fall* will be released in the fall of 2003. A Licensed Professional Counselor, he lives with Susan Onebane O'Neal, his three cats and his two Golden Retrievers, Sam and Susie.

Bibliography

Artwork
Lazarus, Frances Baruch
La Celestine, ("Black Widow") Pablo Picasso, Block 1602, 1971

Books/Articles
DeCastellejo, Irene, *Knowing Woman*, Shambala, 1997.
  (N.Y.: Harper & Row, 1974)
Edinger, Edward, *The Psyche on Stage*, Inner City, 2000
    Archetype of the Apocalypse, Open Court, 1999
Eliot, T. S. *The Waste Land*, Collected Poems, Harcourt, Bruce
Esquire magazine, 1999
Gugenbuhl-Craig, Adolph, *Marriage—Dead or Alive?*
  Spring Publishers, 1977
Hamilton, Edith, *Mythology*, Little, Brown and Company, 1940
Heyraud, Joyce King, *Psychological Perspectives* (No. 40, 2000), a review of
  American Beauty, Los Angeles
Johnson, Robert, *We, She, He*, Harper and Row, 1989
Jung, Carl, *Modern Man in Search of a Soul*, Harcourt, Brace, 1933
    The Archetypes and the Collective Unconscious,
    Princeton, 1959, CW 9i
    Seminar on Dream Analysis, Dec. 1928, p. 633;
    Princeton, 1984
    Symbols of Transformation, (CW 5, p.354, p.551)
    Princeton, 1956
    Memories, Dreams and Reflections, Vintage Books, Random
    House, 1965

Neumann, Erich, *The Great Mother*, Bollingen, Princeton, 1963

Sabini, M., ed. *The Earth Has a Soul*, The Nature Writings of
    C. G. Jung, North Atlantic, 2002

Sanford, Jack, *Invisible Partners*, Paulist Press, 1980
        Between People, Paulist Press, 1982

Sharp, Daryl, *Dear Gladys*, Inner City, 1994
        Digesting Jung, Inner City, 2001

Turow, Scott, *Personal Injuries*, FSG, 1999

Von Franz, Marie-Louise, *Way of the Dream*, Shambala, 1994
        The Feminine in Fairy Tales, Shambala, 1972,
        1993, (N.Y. Spring Publications, 1972)
        The Golden Ass, Shambala, 1993
        Anima and Animus, Inner City, 2002

Whitehead, Barbara, *Why There are No Good Men Left, The Romantic Plight of the New Single Woman*, Broadway Books, 2003

Film/Video

Remembering Jung, with Marie-Louise von Franz

Music/Opera

Floyd, Carlisle, *Cold Sassy Tree*

Verdi, Giuseppe, *Nabucco;* Chorus, *Va Pensiero;* Ambrosian Opera Chorus and Philharmonia Orchestra, Riccardo Muti, conductor, Angel SCLX 3850

Index

A

Age of Aquarius, 59-60
   The new Aeon, 59
American Beauty
   as American film, 5, 21; screenplay, 2
   best original screenplay, 3
   quotes from screen notes, 12
   the writer's script, 2, 53, 62
   as dysfunction of American
     relationships, 5, 19, 33-35, 37
   central image, 1
   the rose, 1-2, 6, 20, 80
   as subject matter, 6, 43-44, 51, 81
   as work, 26, 27-28, 42-43, 51, 67-68
   picture of, 26a
American family life 1, 5, 8, 80
   "Happily ever after" 2, 15, 38-39
   shadow side of, 1, 8, 64-65
American shadow, 65
Anima, 5, 7, 10, 21, 31, 33, 51, 52
   as sexual projection, 6, 7, 8, 9, 10
Animus, 6, 7, 16, 17, 31-32, 41, 45, 52,
   71, 79-81
   and "shoulds," p 31, ff 85
Anima and animus, 8, 19, 21, 22, 32, 34,
   37, 40, 46, 47, 50, 53, 64, 77, 82
Angela, 3, 7, 10-13, 63-70
   as American feminine shadow, 65
Angela and Lester, 7, 10-13
Anthony Quinn, 26
Aphrodite, 7, 24, 80
   and love, 22, 24
   and sexuality, 22-26
   and beauty, 24-25, 60
   picture of, 7
   as goddess of relationships, 22, 61
   myth of Psyche and Amor, 61
Ares, God of War, 24
archetype(s) 6, 19, 22, 41, 43, 71, 77, 79
Archetype of the Apocalypse, 5
archetypal energy, 3
astrology, 59-60
Age of Aquarius, 59-60
astrological signs:
   Aquarius, 59
   Cancer, 40

   Gemini, 60
   Jupiter, 5, 60
   Mercury, 59
   Saturn, 60, 77
   Saturn-Jupiter dance, 60-61

B

Ball, Alan (scriptwriter)
   interviews with, 2, 3
Barbara, the Colonel's wife, 3, 9, 33, 65,
   77-78
Baruch, Frances, *Lazarus*, 27
beauty, 3, 5, 10, 12-13, 25, 64, 71-72, 73
   notion of, 12-13, 60
Book of Genesis, 45
"Bridges," 70
Buddy and Carolyn, 3, 7, 33, 80
Burnham family, 3

C

Carolyn, 3, 6, 7, 12, 16, 20, 34, 77-80,
   89-90
Carolyn and Lester, 5-7, 18, 19, 30, 34,
   77, 83
Carolyn and Buddy, the Realtor, 3, 7, 33,
   80
characters of movie, listed, 3
The "Colonel" (Frank Fitts) 3, 8-9,
   77-78, 84-90
The Colonel and Barbara, 3, 9, 33,
   77-78, 84
The Colonel and Ricky, 8-9, 65-72
The Colonel as Shadow, 8, 83, 86
   Nazi plate and swastika, 9, 71
communication, (relatedness), 31-34,
   46-47, 63-64, 70-71
complexes, 33-34
   mother complex, 28
Cold Sassy Tree, Carlisle Floyd (opera),
   39-40
conflict, 33, 37
consciousness, 41, 54, 67, 73
creative, creative work, 2, 4, 58
   defined, 2

D
Dante, 76
de Castellejo, Irene, *Knowing Woman*,
  "Bridges", 70
the depths, 1-4, 20, 24, 31
  depth psychology, 1
Disney, Walt, 2
dreams, 29-30, 54
Dream Analysis, C.G. Jung. 25, 34-36

E
Edinger, Edward, *The Psyche on Stage*, 42
  The Archetype of the Apocalypse, 5
ego, 3, 47-49, 53, 54, 62, 67, 82, 85, 88
  ego strength, 54, 74
  four types of ego, Fritz Kunkel, 78
Eliot, T.S., *The Waste Land*, 5
enantiodromia, 45, 61
Eros, 73, 80-82
  dark side of, 78
Evans, Nicholas, *The Loop*, 58
Evil Spirit of Passion, 25-26
extravert, 44, 89

F
fantasy, 1, 2, 7, 10-12, 41-46
father(s), 41, 50, 65-66
  article on, 41
fear,
  Jung's quote on, 48-50, 57-59, 66
  as poison, 48
  as spirit of evil, 48
The Feminine in Fairy Tales, Marie-Louise
  von Franz, 45
the feminine, 30, 47, 80, 82, 83, 90
feminine side, 22, 85-86
Florence (Italy), 75-76, 76a
Floyd, Carlisle, *Cold Sassy Tree*
  (Opera), 39-40
Fonda, Jane, 45-47
Franz, Gilda, 25

G
God, 2, 3, 4, 30, 43, 45, 79, 85-86
The Golden Ass, Marie-Louise von Franz,
  21
Gugenbuhl-Craig, Adolph, *Marriage—
  Dead or Alive?*, 45
Gus, 9, 34

Gus and Canille, 34

H
Hamilton, Edith, *Mythology*, 24
hero, heroine, 3, 48-49, 52, 58, 61,
  74, 87
  Jung's definition, 45
Heyraud, Joyce, *Psychological
  Perspectives*, 75, 80
Hollywood, 2
homosexuality, 8-9

I
The I Ching, Hexagram #11, 82, 84,
  87-88
images,
  in artwork, 23
individuality, 27-29
introverts, 44, 62
The Invisible Partners, Jack Sanford, 51

J
Jane character, 3-6, 10, 62
Jane and Angela, 62-63, 69
Jane and Ricky, 4-5, 62-65, 68ff, 89-90
Jesus, quote from, 83
J.B. (Jim Berkeley) character, 8
Jim character, 8
Johnson, Robert, *We*, 44; *She*, 61
journal, 2, 73
Jung, Carl, 17, 20-21, 42, 43, 70, 73,
  85-86
  on fear, 48-51, 57-59, 66
  and *Siegfried*, 86
  Memories, Dreams and Reflections. 86
  Modern Man in Search of a Soul, 4
  Dream Analysis, 34-36
  Symbols of Transformation, CW5,
    56-58
  The Archetypes and the Collective
    Unconscious, CW 9i, 77
  Red Book, 73
Jungian Analysis, 18
Jungian Psychology, 1

K
Knowing Woman, Irene de Castellejo,
  "Bridges", 70
Kunkel, Fritz, (ego types described), 78

L

Lazarus, artwork, 78
  the picture of, 27
Lester, 3, 6-8, 5-9, 16, 22, 30-31, 34, 78, 91
Lester and Angela, 7, 10-12, 13
Lester and Carolyn, 5, 7, 8, 19, 30, 34, 72, 77, 83
Lester and Ricky, 66-68, 91
The Loop, Nicholas Evans, 58,
love, 22, 24, 45
  levels of, 24

M

Marilyn Monroe, 30-31
Marriage—Dead or Alive? Adolph Gugenbuhl-Craig, 45
masculine, 9, 51
  masculinity, 16-17
  masculine energy, 40
  inferior masculine, 71,
  masculine creative power, 77, 83
  masculine rage, 9, 89-90
  masculine Shadow, 8, 9
  masculine Shadow's effect on women, 9
Memories, Dreams and Reflections, Carl Jung, 87
mid-life, 5, 20
mirror, as symbol, 29
Modern Man in Search of a Soul, Carl Jung, 4
mother complex, 28

N

Nabucco, Giuseppe Verdi, (Opera), 1, 40-41
  chorus: *Va, Pensiero,* 1, 59
  the march, 40
Neumann, Erich, *The Great Mother,* 21

O

objectivity, 40, 89
Oprah, magazine, 45
O'Reilly, Bill (Fox News), 21

P

participation mystique, 34-37, 89
Pablo Picasso, 47
Personal Injuries, Scott Turow, 14-16
playing catch, 32-34, 43-44, 64, 66, 81
projection(s), 6, 11-12, 20, 28, 42
  as affairs, 6, 37
  in art, 21
  family projection, e.g. "the ideal family", 27, 35, 36, 37
  of the anima, 6, 10, 12
  of the animus, 17
  of the shadow, 7, 8, 84, 86
The Psyche on Stage, Edward Edinger, 42
psyche, 21
  objective psyche, 89
Psychological Perspectives (number 40, 2000), a review
  of *American Beauty* by Joyce King Heyraud, 76, 81
  quoting Jung, 20

Q

Quinn, Anthony, 26

R

reality, 7, 10, 14, 22
relationships, 22-24
Renaissance, 76-77
Ricky, 4-5, 8, 61, 62, 62-74, 85
  statement on the benevolent force in life, 4-5, 69, 71-74, 90
Ricky and the Colonel, 65-74
Ricky and Jane, 5, 62-65, 68ff, 69-70, 90-91
Ricky and Lester, 66-68, 91
romantic, 22, 27
romance, 42, 45
romanticism, 27
roses, 1-2, 5, 22-27, 30, 33, 68, 69
  American Beauty rose, 6, 18
  as Eros, 23-24
  as heavy feeders, 26
  hybrid tea, 6, 23, 26a
  old fashioned roses, 22a
  red roses, 1, 80
  rose petals, 6; rose petal fantasies, 68
  symbol of, 6, 22, 81
  with thorns, 22-23

S

Sanford, Jack, 85
   The Invisible Partners, 51
   Between People, 32, 32-34,
     (chapter 2 throughout)
secrets, 36
The Self, 33-34, 71-73, 77
sex, sexuality; 7-10, 13-15, 37
   Lester's projection on Angela, 37,
passion
   Venus, goddess of love and sexuality, 37
sexual fantasy, 5, 6, 10, 11, 12, 13, 14, 16
Shadow, 3, 8, 71, 84, 86
She, Robert Johnson, 61
Snow White, 29
soul, 22, 24
   as feminine, 77, 80
Symbols of Transformation, Carl Jung, 56-58
sun image, (Florence), 75

T

Teenager's Nightmare, 14
The Great Mother, Erich Neumann, 21
Turner, Ted, 45-47
Turow, Scott, *Personal Injuries*, 14-16

U

unconscious, 2, 33, 37
   creative, 2
   as work, task, 2, 3
   identifying with, 26, 89
   possessed by, 89

V

Verdi, 1, 39, 58
   The spirit of Verdi's music, 39
   Verdi's music as uplifting, 39,
   Va Pensiero chorus 1, 58
VonFranz, Marie-Louise, 21, 29-30, 33, 38, 46, 49, 52, 58
   The Way of the Dream, 29-30
   The Feminine in Fairy Tales, 46
   The Golden Ass of Apuleius, 21

W

The Way of the Dream,
   Marie-Louise von Franz, 29-30
We, Robert Johnson, 45
Why There are No Good Men Left,
   Barbara Whitehead, 23, 46

Z

zinnias, 40a
Zorba, 26